easy
Plus-Size Knits

50 Knit and Crochet Styles

FamilyCircle®
easy
Plus-Size Knits

50 Knit and Crochet Styles

Sixth&Spring Books
New York

Sixth&Spring Books
233 Spring Street
New York, NY 10013

Editorial Director
Trisha Malcolm

Art Director
Chi Ling Moy

Book Editor
Miriam Gold

Copy Editor
Jean Guirguis

Yarn Editor
Veronica Manno

Technical Editors
Carla Scott
Pat Harste

Book Manager
Michelle Lo

Production Manager
David Joinnides

President and Publisher, Sixth&Spring Books
Art Joinnides

Family Circle Magazine

Editor-in-Chief
Susan Kelliher Ungaro

Executive Editor
Barbara Winkler

Creative Director
Diane Lamphron

Library of Congress Catalog-in-Publication Data
Family circle easy plus-size knits: 50 knit and crochet styles
        p.cm.
    ISBN 1-931543-58-5
        1. Knitting--Patterns. 2. Overweight--Clothing. 3. Overweight men--Clothing. I.
    Title: At head of title: Family Circle. II. Malcolm, Trisha, 1960- III. Family Circle.

TT825 .E27957 2004
746.43'20432--dc22

Table of Contents

Keep It Casual

Slip into these relaxed knits for easy-going good looks.

Cold-Weather Classic

Perfect for the woman on the go, this Victoria Mayo design works anywhere, anytime. A roomy fit and drop sleeves provide the comfort, while a mock turtleneck and deep ribbing add the style. "Cold-Weather Classic" first appeared in the Fall '98 issue of *Family Circle Easy Knitting*.

MATERIALS
- *Colourmates* by Naturally/S.R. Kertzer 1³/₄oz/50g skeins each approx 55yd/50m (wool) 19 (20, 22, 23, 25) balls #0803 teal
- One pair size 10¹/₂ (6.5mm) knitting needles OR SIZE TO OBTAIN GAUGE
- Size 10¹/₂ (6.5mm) circular needle, 16"/40cm long

SIZES
Sized for Woman's Large (X-Large, 1X, 2X,3X). Shown in size X-Large.

FINISHED MEASUREMENTS
- Bust 48 (52, 56, 60, 64)"/122 (132, 142, 152, 162.5)cm
- Length 25¹/₂ (26, 26¹/₂, 27, 27¹/₂)"/64.5 (66, 67.5, 68.5, 70)cm
- Upper arm 19 (20, 20, 21, 22)"/48 (51, 51, 53, 56)cm

GAUGE
14 sts and 18 rows to 4"/10cm over St st using size 10¹/₂ (6.5mm) needles.
TAKE TIME TO CHECK YOUR GAUGE.

RIB PATTERN
(multiple of 3 sts plus 2)
Row 1 (RS) K2, *p1, k2; rep from * to end.
Row 2 K the knit sts and p the purl sts.
Rep row 2 for rib pat.

BACK
With size 10¹/₂ (6.5mm) needles, cast on 92 (98, 104, 113, 119) sts. Work in rib pat for 3"/7.5cm, end with a WS row. K next row on RS, dec 8 (7, 6, 8, 7) sts evenly across—84 (91, 98, 105, 112) sts. Cont in St st until piece measures 16 (16, 16¹/₂, 16¹/₂ , 16¹/₂)"/40.5 (40.5, 42, 42, 42)cm from beg.

Armhole shaping
Bind off 6 (7, 7, 8, 8) sts at beg of next 2 rows—72 (77, 84, 89, 96) sts. Work even until armhole measures 8¹/₂ (9, 9, 9¹/₂, 10)"/21.5 (23, 23, 24, 25.5)cm, end with a WS row.

Neck shaping
Next row (RS) Work 25 (27, 30, 32, 35) sts, join 2nd ball of yarn and bind off center 22 (23, 24, 25, 26) sts, work to end. Working both sides at once, bind off from each neck edge 4 sts once. Bind off rem 21 (23, 26, 28, 31) sts each side for shoulders.

FRONT
Work same as back until armhole measures 7 (7¹/₂, 7¹/₂, 8, 8¹/₂)"/17.5 (19, 19, 20, 21.5)cm, end with a WS row.

Neck shaping
Next row (RS) Work 28 (30, 33, 35, 38) sts, join 2nd ball of yarn and bind off center 16 (17, 18, 19, 20) sts, work to end. Working both sides at once, bind off from each neck edge 3 sts once, 2 sts once, 1 st twice. When same length as back to shoulder, bind off rem 21 (23, 26, 28, 31) sts each side for shoulders.

SLEEVES
With size 10¹/₂ (6.5mm) needles, cast on 41 (44, 44, 44, 47) sts. Work in rib pat 3"/7.5cm, end with a WS row. K next row on RS, inc 2 sts—43 (46, 46, 46, 49) sts. Cont in St st, inc 1 st each side every 4th row 6 (6, 6, 13, 13) times, every 6th row 6 (6, 6, 1, 1) times—67 (70, 70, 74, 77) sts. Work even until piece measures 18¹/₂"/47cm from beg. Bind off all sts.

FINISHING
Block pieces very lightly. Sew shoulder seams.
Mock turtleneck
With RS facing and circular needle, pick up and k 72 (75, 75, 78, 81) sts evenly around neck edge. Join and work in k2, p1 rib pat for 4¹/₂"/12.5cm. Bind off loosely in rib. Set in sleeves, sewing last 1³/₄ (2, 2, 2¹/₄, 2¹/₄)"/4.5 (5, 5, 5.5, 5.5)cm at top of sleeve to 6 (7, 7, 8, 8) bound-off armhole sts. Sew side and sleeve seams.

(Schematics on page 116)

8 Keep it Casual

My Fair Lady

for advanced knitters

Winter would not be winter without a cozy Fair Isle sweater to fend off the bitter days and blustery nights. Imagine an evening by the fire in this gorgeous design, featuring a cowl neck and knuckle-skimming sleeves worked in two strands for a heather effect. "My Fair Lady" first appeared in the Winter '99/'00 issue of *Family Circle Easy Knitting*.

MATERIALS

- *Nature Spun Sport* by Brown Sheep Yarn Co., 1¾oz/50g balls, each approx 184yd/170m (wool)
  - 9 (9, 10, 11) balls in #N03 lt grey (A)
  - 7 (7, 8, 8) balls in #880 med grey (B)
  - 4 (4, 5, 5) balls in #N42 dk purple (C)
  - 3 (3, 4, 4) balls each in #601 black (D) and #N80 dark purple (E)
- One pair each sizes 7 and 9 (4.5 and 5.5mm) needles OR SIZE TO OBTAIN
- Size 7 (4.5mm) circular needle, 16"/40cm long

SIZES

Sized for Small/Medium (Large, X-Large, XX-Large). Shown in size Small/Medium.

FINISHED MEASUREMENTS

- Bust 42 (46, 50, 55)"/106.5 (116.5, 127, 139.5)cm
- Length 29 (30¼, 31, 32)"/74 (77, 78.5, 81)cm
- Upper arm 15 (17, 19, 20½)"/38 (43, 48.5, 52)cm

GAUGES

- 17 sts and 24 rows to 4"/10cm over St st using larger needles and 2 strands of yarn.
- 18 sts and 22 rows to 4"/10cm over St st and chart pats using larger needles and 2 strands of yarn.

TAKE TIME TO CHECK YOUR GAUGES.

Note

Work with 2 strands of yarn held tog throughout in the foll color combinations:
Color 1 = 1 strand each A and B
Color 2 = 2 strands D
Color 3 = 1 strand each C and E
Color 4 = 1 strand each C and D
Color 5 = 2 strands A

BACK

With smaller needles and Color 1, cast on 108 (118, 128, 138) sts. Work in k1, p1 rib for 1¼"/3cm. Change to larger needles and work in St st for 24 (26, 26, 28) rows. Dec 1 st each side on next row, then every 12th row 6 times more—94 (104, 114, 124) sts.

Note Read to end of piece before beg to knit.

Beg chart 1

Row 1 (RS) Beg with st 5 (2, 6, 3) work to st 14, work 7-st rep (sts 8 to 14) 12 (13, 15, 16) times. Cont as established through chart row 6.

Beg chart 2

Row 1 (RS) Beg with st 4 work to st 15, work 10-st rep (sts 6 to 15) 8 (9, 10, 11) times, work sts 16 to 17. Cont as established through chart row 10, then rep rows 1-12.

Beg chart 3

Row 1 (RS) Work as for chart 1. Cont as established through row 6. Change to Color 3 and cont in St st to end of piece, AT SAME TIME, when piece measures 19 (19½, 19½, 20)"/48.5 (49.5, 49.5, 50.5)cm from beg, end with a WS row.

Raglan armhole shaping

Bind off 4 (4, 4, 5) sts at beg of next 2 rows. Dec 1 st each side every other row 16 (22, 30, 34) times, every 4th row 6 (4, 1, 0) times. Bind off rem 42 (44, 44, 46) sts for back neck.

FRONT

Work as for back until armhole measures 7¼ (8, 8¾, 9¼)"/18.5 (20.5, 22.5, 23.5)cm, end with a WS row.

Neck shaping

Next row (RS) Cont raglan shaping, bind off center 18 (20, 20, 22) sts for neck, and working both sides at once, bind off from each neck edge 4 sts once, 2 sts 4 times. When armhole measures 9¼ (10, 10¾, 11¼)"/23.5 (25.5, 27, 28.5)cm), bind off rem sts each side.

LEFT SLEEVE

With smaller needles and Color 1, cast on 50 (52, 52, 54) sts. Work in k1, p1 rib for 1¼"/3cm. Change to larger needles.

Note Read to end of directions before beg to knit. Work in St st for 6 rows. Work 22 rows of chart 4 twice, then work row 1 once more, then work 1 row with Color 1, then 6 rows chart 1, 12 rows chart 2, 6 rows chart 3, 12 rows chart 5, 2 rows Color 5, 6 rows chart 1, 12 rows chart 2, 6 rows chart 3, then cont with Color 3 to end of piece, AT SAME TIME, inc 1 st each side (working inc sts into pat) every 8th (6th, 4th, 4th) row 5 (6, 9, 14) times, every 10th (8th, 6th, 6th) row 5 (6, 8,

(Continued on page 117)

By the Fire

for intermediate knitters

This lush chevron-striped vest evokes the rich texture and resonant colors of Turkish kilim rugs. Unmistakably a Brandon Mably design, it's a distinctive combination of rustic ease and sophisticated polish. "By the Fire" first appeared in the Holiday '02 issue of *Family Circle Easy Knitting*.

MATERIALS

- ▢ *Lurex Shimmer* by Rowan Yarns, .88oz/25g balls, each approx 103yd/95m (viscose/polyester)
    6 balls each in #330 copper (A), #335 bronze (B)
    4 balls each in #334 black (C), #331 claret (D)
- ▢ *Rowan Spun 4-ply* by Rowan Yarns, .88oz/25g balls, each approx 160yd/147m (wool)
    4 balls each in #705 spiced orange (E), #703 rum (I)
    2 balls each in #709 pine green (F), #708 midnight blue (H), #712 jade (K)
    3 balls each in #706 rosewood (G), #707 leaf green (J))
- ▢ Size 6 (4mm) circular needle, 40"/100cm long OR SIZE NEEDED TO OBTAIN GAUGE

SIZES

Sized for one size.

FINISHED MEASUREMENTS

- ▢ Bust (closed) 56"/142cm
- ▢ Length 22¼"/56.5cm

GAUGE

24 sts and 32 rows to 4"/10cm over St st using 2 strands of each yarn held tog foll chart using larger needles.
TAKE TIME TO CHECK YOUR GAUGE.

Notes

1 Work with 2 strands of yarn held tog throughout.
2 Fronts are worked foll chart. Back is worked in stripes.

BACK

With smaller needles and 1 strand each A & E (AE) held tog, cast on 170 sts. Work in St st for 7 rows. K next row on WS for turning ridge. Change to larger needles and cont in stripe pat as foll: 8 rows AE, 1 row AB, 1 row DG, 1 row CH, 1 row AJ, 12 rows DG, 1 row CH, 1 row AE, 1 row BJ, 1 row CC, 8 rows BJ, 1 row DE, 1 row CC, 1 row BI, 1 row DG, 12 rows CH, 1 row AF, 1 row DG, 1 row DJ, 1 row CK, 8 rows AK, 1 row BC, 1 row DG, 1 row BJ, 1 row BH, 12 rows DJ, 1 row CH, 1 row CI, 1 row CF, 1 row AG, 8 rows BI. Piece measures approx 12¼"/31cm from beg.

Armhole shaping

Bind off 7 sts at beg of next 2 rows, dec 1 st each side every other row 13 times—130 sts, AT SAME TIME, cont in stripe pat as foll: 1 row AJ, 1 row BG, 1 row AE, 1 row BC, 12 rows AK, 1 row DG, 1 row AF, 1 row CJ, 1 row CC, 8 rows DG, 1 row BI, 1 row AE, 1 row BH, 1 row DJ, 12 rows CH, 1 row BG, 1 row AE, 1 row CK, 1 row DG, 8 rows DI, 1 row DK, 1 row CH, 1 row DI, 1 row DG, 12 rows BJ, 1 row CF, 1 row BF, 1 row DG, 1 row BJ, then complete piece with DG. Working this stripe sequence, work even until there are 78 rows in armhole and armhole measures 9½"/24cm.

Shoulder shaping

Bind off 13 sts at beg of next 2 rows, 14 sts at beg of next 2 rows, 11 sts at beg of next 2 rows, 7 sts at beg of next 2 rows, AT SAME TIME, bind off center 32 sts for neck and working both sides at once, bind off 4 sts from each neck edge once.

RIGHT FRONT

With smaller needles and 1 strand each A & E (AE) held tog, cast on 85 sts. Work in St st for 7 rows. K next row on WS for turning ridge. Change to larger needles.

Beg chart pat

Row 1 (RS) Beg with row 1 of chart, work in color pat foll chart. Cont to foll chart in this way through row 57.

Armhole shaping

Next row (WS) Bind off 7 sts, work to end. Cont to foll chart dec 1 st at armhole edge every other row 13 times AT SAME TIME, on row 61, dec 1 st at beg of row (neck edge) and rep neck dec every 4th row once, every 3rd row twice, then every 4th row 16 times—45 sts. Cont to foll chart through row 137.

Shoulder shaping

Next row (WS) Bind off 13 sts, work to end. Cont to bind off 14 sts from shoulder edge once, 11 sts once, 7 sts once.

LEFT FRONT

Work color pat as a mirror image of right front chart (that is, the colors match at center front) and reverse all shaping.

FINISHING

Block pieces to measurements. Sew shoulder seams. With smaller needles and 1 strand AK, pick up and k 132 sts evenly around armhole edge. Bind off purlwise.

FRONT BANDS

Using circular needle and 1 strand AE alternated with 1 strand CK, pick up and k 315 sts as foll: 3 sts CK, * 3 sts AE, 3 sts CK; rep from * to end. Working in St st in colors as established,

(Continued on page 118)

Cardigan Clout

Trends come and go, but the good old-fashioned cardigan outlasts them all. Norah Gaughan integrates eye-catching cables and practical ribbing for a roomy-yet-flattering cut that's fine for any body type. "Cardigan Clout" first appeared in the Fall '00 issue of *Family Circle Easy Knitting*.

MATERIALS

- *Star* by Classic Elite Yarns, 1¾oz/50g, each approx 112yd/103m (cotton/lycra) 13 (15, 16) hanks in #5148 blue
- One pair each sizes 4 and 6 (3.5 and 4mm) OR SIZE TO OBTAIN GAUGE
- Cable needle
- Six ¾"/19mm buttons

SIZES

Sized for Large/X-Large (1X/2X, 3X). Shown in size Large/X-Large.

FINISHED MEASUREMENTS

- Bust (buttoned) 49¾ (56¼, 61¼)"/126 (142.5, 155.5)cm
- Length 24 (24½, 25)"/61 (62, 63.5)cm
- Upper arm 20 (21, 22)"/51 (53, 56)cm

GAUGE

22 sts and 30 rows to 4"/10cm over chart pat using larger needles.
TAKE TIME TO CHECK YOUR GAUGE.

STITCH GLOSSARY

4-st RC

Sl 2 sts to cn and hold to *back*, k2, k2 from cn.

BACK

With smaller needles, cast on 134 (152, 164) sts. Work in k2, p2 rib for 1½"/4cm. Change to larger needles. K 1 row, p 1 row.

*Beg chart 1

Row 1 (RS) Beg as indicated, work to end of chart (center), work chart back from left to right, end as indicated. Cont in pat as established until 4 rows of chart 1 have been worked 13 times. Work in St st over all sts for 2 rows.

Beg chart 2

Row 1 (RS) Beg as indicated, work to end of chart (center), work chart back from left to right, end as indicated. Cont in pat as established until 4 rows of chart 2 have been worked 13 times. Work in St st over all sts for 2 rows.

Rep from * (108 rows) until piece measures 23 (23½, 24)"/58.5 (59.5, 61)cm from beg, end with a WS row.

Neck shaping

Next row (RS) Work 52 (61, 67) sts, join 2nd ball of yarn and bind off center 30 sts, work to end. Working both sides at once, bind off 5 sts from each neck edge twice. Work even until piece measures 24 (24½, 25)"/61 (62, 63.5)cm from beg. Bind off rem 42 (51, 57) sts each side for shoulders.

LEFT FRONT

With smaller needles, cast on 67 (76, 82) sts. Work in k2, p2 rib for 1½"/4cm. Change to larger needles. K 1 row, p 1 row.

Beg chart I

Row 1 (RS) Beg as indicated, work to end of chart. Cont in pat as established as for back until piece measures 20 (20½, 21)"/51 (52, 53.5)cm from beg, end with a RS row.

Neck shaping

Next row (WS) Bind off 6 sts (neck edge), work to end. Cont to bind off from neck edge 4 sts once, 3 sts twice, 2 sts 3 times and 1 st 3 times. Work even until same length as back. Bind off rem 42 (51, 57) sts for shoulder.

RIGHT FRONT

Work to correspond to left front, reversing chart pats as foll: Beg at end of chart (center) work chart backwards from left to right, end as indicated.

Reverse neck shaping by dec sts at beg of RS rows.

SLEEVES

With smaller needles, cast on 62 sts. Work in k2, p2 rib for 1½"4cm. Change to larger needles. K 1 row, p 1 row.

Beg chart pat

Row 1 (RS) Beg as indicated for sleeve, work to end of chart (center), work chart back from left to right, end as indicated for sleeve. Cont in pat as established, working rows as for back, AT SAME TIME, inc 1 st each side (working inc sts into chart pat) every 4th row 14 (23, 29) times, every 6th row 10 (4, 0) times—110 (116, 120) sts. Work even until piece measures 18"/45.5cm from beg. Bind off all sts.

(Continued on page 119)

Zigzag

for intermediate knitters

Cynthia Yanok Wise's T-length tie-front vest is a flirty urban design that marries ease and style. The zigzag cabling pops out of the understated reverse stockinette-stitch background for a striking multidimensional effect. "Zigzag" first appeared in the Winter '01 issue of *Family Circle Easy Knitting*.

MATERIALS

- *Highlander* by Garnstudio/Aurora Yarns 1³⁄₄oz/50g balls, each approx 88yd/80m (wool/nylon) 15 (17, 18, 20) balls in #03 gold
- One pair size 11 (8mm) needles OR SIZE TO OBTAIN GAUGE
- One set (4) size 11 (8mm) dpn
- Two size 9 (5.5mm) dpn
- Stitch holders
- Cable needle (cn)

SIZES

Sized for Large (X-large, 1X, 2X). Shown in size Large.

FINISHED MEASUREMENTS

- Bust 51 (57, 61, 67)"/130 (145, 155, 170)cm
- Length 45¹⁄₂ (45¹⁄₂, 46, 46¹⁄₂)"/115.5 (115.5, 117, 118)cm

GAUGES

- 14 sts and 15 rows to 4"/10cm over zigzag pat using size 11 (8mm) needles.
- 11 sts and 15 rows to 4"/10cm over reverse St st using size 11 (8mm) needles.
  TAKE TIME TO CHECK YOUR GAUGES.

STITCH GLOSSARY

3-st RC Sl 1 st to cn and hold to *back*, k2, p1 from cn.

3-st LC Sl 2 sts to cn and hold to *front*, p1, k2 from cn.

ZIGZAG PATTERN

(over 20 sts)

Row 1 (WS) K3, p2, k3, p4, k3, p2, k3. **Row 2 (RS)** [P2, 3-st RC] twice, [3-st LC, p2] twice. **Row 3 and all WS rows** K the knit and p the purl sts. **Row 4** P1, [3-st RC, p2] twice, 3-st LC, p2, 3-st LC, p1. **Row 6** [3-st RC, p2] twice, [p2, 3-st LC] twice. **Row 8** [3-st LC, p2] twice, [p2, 3-st RC] twice. **Row 10** P1, [3-st LC, p2] twice,

3-st RC, p2, 3-st RC, p1. **Row 12** [P2, 3-st LC] twice, [3-st RC, p2] twice.
Rep rows 1-12 for zigzag pat.

BACK

Cast on 80 (88, 94, 102) sts. **Row 1 (WS)** P3, k5 (9, 12, 16), work zigzag pat over 20 sts, k9, p6, k9, work zigzag pat over 20 sts, k5 (9, 12, 16), p3. Cont in pats as established until piece measures 35"/89cm from beg.

Armhole shaping

Next row (RS) K3, p2tog, work to last 5 sts, p2tog, k3. Work 1 row even. Rep last 2 rows 4 (6, 8, 10) times more—70(74, 76, 80) sts. Work even until armhole measures 10¹⁄₂ (10¹⁄₂, 11, 11¹⁄₂)"/26.5 (26.5, 28, 29)cm.

Neck and shoulder shaping

Next row (RS) Work 26 (28, 29, 31) sts, p2tog, join 2nd ball of yarn and bind off center 14 sts, p2tog, work to end. Working both sides at once, dec 1 st from each neck edge on next row. Leave rem 26 (28, 29, 31,) sts on holders for each shoulder.

LEFT FRONT

Cast on 40 (44, 47, 51) sts. **Row 1 (WS)** P3, k5 (9, 12, 16), work zigzag pat over 20 sts, k9, p3. Cont in pats as established until piece measures 35"/89cm from beg.

Armhole and neck shaping

Next row (RS) K3, p2tog, work to last 5 sts, p2tog, k3. Cont to dec 1 st in this way every other row at armhole edge 4 (6, 8, 10) times more and dec 1 st at neck edge every 4th row 8 times—26 (28, 29, 31) sts. When same length as back, sl rem sts to a holder for shoulder.

RIGHT FRONT

Work as for left front reversing pat placements and shaping.

FINISHING

Block pieces to measurements. With WS of pieces tog, using 3-needle bind-off method, leaving 3 sts from each neck edge on holders, bind off the 23 (25, 26, 28) rem sts from corresponding shoulders tog. Then with WS tog and corresponding 3 sts at one neck edge, p 1 st from front needle tog with 1 st from back needle—3 sts. Cont on these 3 sts until band fits to center of back neck. Leave sts on holder and rep for other side of neckband. Weave sts tog at center back neck using Kitchener st (see page 120). Sew band to center back neck. Sew side seams.

I-cords

With smaller dpn, cast on 2 sts. *K2. Slide sts

(Continued on page 120)

Stripe it Up

for beginner knitters

Discreet stripes in gorgeous pinks and purples along with a modern slip-stitch pattern manage to make JCA's down-to-earth vest an exercise in both subtlety and vibrancy. "Stripe it Up" first appeared in the Winter '00/'01 issue of *Family Circle Easy Knitting*.

MATERIALS

- *Harmony* by Reynolds/JCA, 4oz/125g hanks, each approx 173yd/159m (wool)
  2 (3, 3, 4, 4) hanks in #17 blue purple multi (B)
  1 (2, 2, 3, 3) hanks each in #3 plum (C) and #6 blue (A)
- Sizes 6 and 8 (4 and 5mm) circular needle 29"/74cm long OR SIZE TO OBTAIN GAUGE
- Size 6 (4mm) circular needle 16"/40cm long
- One 1³⁄₄"/45mm toggle button

SIZES

To fit Small (Medium, Large, X-Large, XX-Large). Shown in size Small.

FINISHED MEASUREMENTS

- Bust 38 (40, 44, 48, 52)"/96.5 (101.5, 111.5, 122, 132)cm
- Length 24 (24¹⁄₂, 25, 25¹⁄₂, 26)"/61 (62, 63.5, 65, 66)cm

GAUGE

18 sts and 28 rows to 4"/10cm over pat st using larger needles.
TAKE TIME TO CHECK YOUR GAUGE.

PATTERN STITCH

(over an odd number of sts)
Row 1 (RS) *K1, sl 1 wyib; rep from *, end k1.
Row 2 *P1, k1; rep from *, end p1.
Row 3 Knit.
Row 4 *K1, p1; rep from *, end k1. Work these 4 rows for pat st in the foll color sequence: 4 rows in A, then * 4 rows each in C, B, C, A, B, A; rep from * for stripe pat throughout.

BODY

With smaller 29"/75cm circular needle and A, cast on 173 (181, 197, 217, 233) sts. Working in k1, p1 rib, work 2 rows A, 3 rows B. Change to larger needles and p next WS row with B. Then, cont in pat st and stripe pat until piece measures 16"/40cm from beg.

Divide for back and fronts

Next row (RS) Work 39 (41, 44, 48, 52) sts and place on holder for right front; bind off 8 (8, 10, 12, 12) sts for armhole, work until there are 79 (83, 89, 97, 105) sts from bind-off, leave rem sts on a holder to be worked later. Cont on sts for back only, work 1 row even. Then bind off 3 sts at beg of next 2 (2, 4, 6, 8) rows, 2 sts at beg of next 4 (4, 2, 0, 0) rows then dec 1 st each side every other row 3 (4, 5, 7, 7) times—59 (61, 63, 65, 67) sts. Work even until armholes measure 7¹⁄₂ (8, 8¹⁄₂, 9, 9¹⁄₂)"/19 (20.5, 21.5, 23, 24)cm.

Neck shaping

Next row (RS) Work 24 (25, 25, 26, 26) sts, join another ball of yarn and bind off center 11 (11, 13, 13, 15) sts, work to end. Working both sides at once, bind off 6 sts from each neck edge once. Bind off rem 18 (19, 19, 20, 20) sts each side for shoulders.

LEFT FRONT

Rejoin yarn to last 47 (49, 54, 60, 64) sts and bind off 8 (8, 10, 12, 12) sts for armhole, work to end. Cont to shape armhole binding off from armhole edge 3 sts 1 (1, 2, 3, 4) times, 2 sts 2 (2, 1, 0, 0) times, dec 1 st every other row 3 (4, 5, 7, 7) times and AT SAME TIME, when piece measures 18 (18, 18¹⁄₂, 18¹⁄₂, 19)"/45.5 (45.5, 47, 47, 48)cm from beg, shape neck by dec 1 st from neck edge on next row and every alternate 2nd and 4th row a total of 10 (10, 11, 11, 12) times more. When same length as back, bind off rem 18 (19, 19, 20, 20) sts for shoulders.

RIGHT FRONT

Rejoin yarn to work 39 (41, 44, 48, 52) sts for right front and work to correspond to left front, reversing shaping.

FINISHING

Block to measurements. Sew shoulder seams.

Armhole edging

With RS facing and smaller circular needle and A, pick up and k 82 (87, 93, 98, 104) sts. K 1 rnd. Bind off purlwise.

Front and neck edging

With smaller circular needle and A, beg a lower right front edge, pick up and k 240 (245, 250, 256, 261) sts evenly around inside front and back neck edge, pm at beg of right front neck shaping. **Next row (WS)** Knit to 2 sts before neck marker, k2tog, yo twice, ssk, k

(Continued on page 120)

True Blue

for intermediate knitters

Irina Poludnenko gives the pullover a makeover with this dynamic design worked in one piece. Garter-stitched sleeves and a stockinette-stitched body show off the yarn's pretty palette, while raglan styling accentuates the shoulders. "True Blue" first appeared in the Fall '02 issue of *Family Circle Easy Knitting*.

MATERIALS

- *Chrysalis* by Colinette/Unique Kolours, 3½oz/100g balls, each approx 92yd/84m (cotton/polyamide)
  8 (9, 9, 10) balls in #93 lapis
- One each size 10 (6mm) circular needle 40"/100cm and 16"/40cm long

SIZES

Sized for Woman's Large (1X, 2X, 3X). Shown in size Large.

FINISHED MEASUREMENTS

- Bust 48 (50, 53, 56)"/122 (127, 135, 142)cm
- Length 24 (24½, 25½, 26)"/61 (62, 65, 66)cm
- Upper arm 18 (19, 19¾, 20½)"/45.5 (48, 50, 52)cm

GAUGE

10 sts and 16 rows to 4"/10cm over St st using size 10 (6mm) needles.
TAKE TIME TO CHECK YOUR GAUGE.

NOTE

Pullover is made in one piece beg at lower back edge and ending at lower front edge.

BACK

With longer circular needle, cast on 60 (62, 66, 70) sts. K 1 row. Then beg with a p row, work in St st until piece measures 13 (13, 13½, 13½)"/33 (33, 34, 34)cm from beg, end with a WS row.

Beg sleeves

Next row (RS) Cast on 3 sts, k3, sl next st to cn and hold to *front*, k1, k1 from cn (FT), k to last 2 sts, sl next to cn and hold to *back*, k1, k1 from cn (BT). **Next row (WS)** Cast on 3 sts, k4, p to last 4 sts, k4. **Next row (RS)** Cast on 3 sts, k7, FT, k to last 6 sts, BT, k4. **Next row (WS)** Cast on 3 sts, k8, p to last 8 sts, k8. Cont in this way to cast on 3 sts at beg of next 24 rows and work FT and BT as established and all cast-on sts outside of the FT or RT in garter st. There are 144 (146, 150, 154) sts after all sts are added for sleeves. Cont with these sts without increasing and cont with FT and BT as established for 16 (18, 20, 22) rows more. There are 14 (14, 16, 18) sts between the FT or RT sts.

Back neck shaping

Next row (RS) K63 (64, 65, 66), FT, sl center 14 (14, 16, 18) sts to a holder for neck, join 2nd ball of yarn, BT, k to end. Working both sides at once, work 1 row even. Discontinue FT and BT while shaping neck as foll: **Next row (RS)** K to last 2 sts at neck edge, k2tog; k2tog on other side of neck, k to end. K 1 row. Rep last 2 rows once more—63 (64, 65, 66) sts rem each side.

Front neck shaping

K 4 rows. **Next row (RS)** K61 (62, 63, 64), BT, cast on 1 st at right neck edge; cast on 1 st at left neck edge, FT, k to end. **Next row** K to last 3 sts, purl 3 on first side; p3, k to end on 2nd side. Rep last 2 rows once more. **Next row (RS)** Work in pat as before with BT on first side, cast on 14 (14, 16, 18) sts for neck, work in pat as before with FT on 2nd side. There are 144 (146, 150, 154) sts. Cont to work as established with FT and BT for 12 (14, 16, 18) rows more. Cont pat, bind off 3 sts at beg of next 28 rows—60 (62, 66, 70) sts. Then cont in St st only for 13 (13, 13½, 13½)"/33 (33, 34, 34)cm more. K 1 row on WS. Bind off knitwise.

FINISHING

Block pieces to measurements. Sew side and sleeve seams. With shorter circular needle, pick up and k50 (50, 54, 58) sts evenly around neck edge. P 1 row. Bind off knitwise.

(Schematics on page 121)

Fall Fuzzy

for intermediate knitters

This comfy cardigan will warm you up instantly on a chilly day! Size 13/9mm needles make it chunky and charming, playing up the simplicity of the stockinette and garter design and showcasing the warm autumn hues of the yarn. "Fall Fuzzy" first appeared in the Fall '03 issue of *Family Circle Easy Knitting*.

MATERIALS
- *Luxor* by Skacel Collection, 1¾oz/50g balls, each approx 58yd/50m (wool/acrylic/nylon) 19 (20, 22, 23, 25) balls in #107 red
- One pair each sizes 11 and 13 (8 and 9mm) needles OR SIZE TO OBTAIN GAUGE
- Stitch holders
- Six 1"/25mm buttons

SIZES
Sized for Small (Medium, Large, X-Large, XX-Large). Shown in size Medium.

FINISHED MEASUREMENTS
- Lower edge (closed) 44 (48, 51½, 54, 57¼)"/111.5 (122, 131, 137, 145.5)cm
- Bust (closed) 39½ (44, 46¾, 49¾, 53)"/100 (111.5, 118.5, 126, 134.5)cm
- Length 28½ (29¼, 30, 30¾, 31½)"/72 (74, 76, 78, 80)cm
- Upper arm 17½ (18, 19, 19½, 20¼)"/44.5 (45.5, 48, 49.5, 51.5)cm

GAUGE
11 sts and 16 rows to 4"/10cm over St st using larger needles.
TAKE TIME TO CHECK YOUR GAUGE.

BACK
With smaller needles, cast on 60 (66, 70, 74, 78) sts. Beg with a WS row, k 3 rows. Change to larger needles, and beg with a k row, work in St st until piece measures 4½"/11cm from beg.
Dec row (RS) Dec 1 st each side of row. Rep dec row every 18th row twice more—54 (60, 64, 68, 72) sts. Work even until piece measures 19½ (19¾, 20, 20½, 21)"/49 (50, 51, 52, 53.5)cm from beg.

Armhole shaping
Bind off 6 sts at beg of next 2 rows—42 (48, 52, 56, 60) sts. Work even until armhole measures 9 (9½, 10, 10¼, 10½)"/23 (24, 25, 26, 26.5)cm. Bind off all sts.

Pocket lining
(make 2)
With larger needles, cast on 13 sts. Work in St st for 9¾"/24cm. Place sts on a holder.

LEFT FRONT
With smaller needles, cast on 33 (36, 38, 40, 43) sts. Beg with a WS row, k 3 rows. Change to larger needles. **Next row (RS)** Knit. **Next row (WS)** Sl 1, k4 (for front band), purl to end. Rep last 2 rows until piece measures 4½"/11cm from beg.
Dec row (RS) Dec 1 st (side edge), work to end. Rep dec at side edge every 18th row twice more, AT SAME TIME, when piece measures 8"/20cm from beg, join pocket lining as foll: **Next row (RS)** K8 (11, 12, 14, 16), bind off next 13 sts for pocket opening, work to end. **Next row (WS)** Work to pocket opening, work 13 sts from one pocket lining, work to end. After all side decs, work even on rem 30 (33, 35, 37, 40) sts until same length as back to armhole.

Armhole shaping
Next row (RS) Bind off 6 sts, work to end—24 (27, 29, 31, 34) sts. Work even until armhole measures 4½ (5, 5½, 5¾, 6)"/11.5 (12.5, 13.5, 14.5, 15) cm, end with a RS row.

Neck shaping
Next row (WS) Bind off 6 (6, 7, 7, 8) sts, work to end. Cont to bind off 2 sts from neck edge twice, 1 st twice—12 (15, 16, 18, 20) sts. Work even until armhole measures same as back. Bind off rem sts for shoulder. Place markers for six buttons on band, with the first one at 1½"/4cm from lower edge, the last one at ½"/1.5cm from neck shaping and the others evenly spaced between.

RIGHT FRONT
Work to correspond to left front, reversing all shaping and placement of pocket and forming buttonholes opposite markers by yo, k2tog at 2 sts from front edge for each buttonhole.

SLEEVES
With smaller needles, cast on 28 (28, 30, 30, 32) sts. Beg with a WS row, k 3 rows. Change to larger needles and beg with a k row, work in St st, inc 1 st each side every 6th row 10 (11, 11, 12, 12) times—48 (50, 52, 54, 56) sts. Work even until piece measures 17½ (17¾, 18, 18½, 18¾)"/44 (45, 46, 47, 47.5)cm from beg. Place yarn markers each side of row. Work even for 2"/5cm more. Bind off.

(Continued on page 121)

Red Alert

for intermediate knitters

Designed by Norah Gaughan, this stunning stockinette-stitched pullover with a bias-knit ribbed collar and sleeves makes a bold statement at the office or an evening soiree. "Red Alert" was first featured in the Holiday '03 issue of *Family Circle Easy Knitting*.

MATERIALS

- *Devotion* by Reynolds/JCA, 1³/₄oz/50g balls, each approx 93yd/84m (angora/nylon) 9 (10, 12, 13, 14) balls in #210 red
- Size 8 (5mm) needles OR SIZE NEEDED TO OBTAIN GAUGE

SIZES

Sized for Small (Medium, Large, X-Large, XX-Large). Shown in size Medium.

FINISHED MEASUREMENTS

- Bust 36 (40, 44, 48, 52)"/91.5 (101.5, 111.5, 122, 132)cm
- Length 23¹/₂ (24, 24¹/₂, 25, 25¹/₂)"/60 (61, 62, 63.5, 64.5)cm
- Upper arm 12 (13, 14, 15, 16)"/30.5 (33, 35.5, 38, 40.5)cm

GAUGE

17 sts and 22 rows to 4"/10cm over St st using size 8 (5mm) needles.
TAKE TIME TO CHECK YOUR GAUGE.

BIAS RIB

(multiple of 3 sts)
Row 1 (WS) *P1, k2; rep from * to end. **Row 2** *P1, k2tog, do not sl st off LH needle, k into first st, sl both sts off needle (RT); rep from * to end. **Row 3** K1, *p1, k2; rep from *, end p1, k1. **Row 4** *RT, p1; rep from * to end. **Row 5** *K2, p1; rep from * to end. **Row 6** K1, *p1, RT; rep from *, end p1, k1. Rep rows 1-6 for bias rib.

BACK

Cast on 76 (86, 94, 102, 110) sts. Work in St st until piece measures 14¹/₂"/37cm from beg.

Armhole shaping

Bind off 4 sts at beg of next 0 (2, 2, 2, 2) rows, 3 sts at beg of next 2 (2, 2, 4, 6) rows, 2 sts at beg of next 4 (2, 4, 4, 2) rows, 1 st at beg of next 4 (4, 4, 2, 4) rows—58 (64, 68, 72, 76) sts. Work even until armhole measures 8 (8¹/₂, 9, 9¹/₂, 10)"/20.5 (21.5, 23, 24, 25.5)cm.

Shoulder and neck shaping

Bind off 4 (5, 5, 7, 7) sts at beg of next 2 rows, 4 (5, 6, 6, 7) sts at beg of next 4 rows, AT SAME TIME, bind off center 18 sts and working both sides at once, bind off from each neck edge 4 sts twice.

FRONT

Work as for back until piece measures 20¹/₂ (21, 21¹/₂, 22, 22¹/₂)"/52 (53.5, 54.5, 56, 57)cm from beg.

Neck shaping

Next row (RS) Work 20 (23, 25, 27, 29) sts, join 2nd ball of yarn and bind off center 18 sts, work to end. Working both sides at once, bind off from each neck edge 3 sts once, 2 sts once, 1 st 3 times, AT SAME TIME, when same length as back to shoulders, shape shoulders as for back.

SLEEVES

Cast on 53 sts. **Next row (WS)** P1, work bias rib to last st, p1. Cont in bias rib, working first and last st in St st, until piece measures 4"/10cm from beg, end with a RS row. P next row on WS, dec 13 (11, 9, 7, 5) sts evenly across—40 (42, 44, 46, 48) sts. Work in St st for 1"/2.5cm. Inc 1 st each side of next row, then every 10th (8th, 6th, 6th, 4th) row 4 (4, 2, 6, 1) times more, every 12th (10th, 8th, 8th, 6th) row 1 (2, 5, 2, 8) times—52 (56, 60, 64, 68) sts. Work even until piece measures 15¹/₂"/39.5cm from beg.

Cap shaping

Bind off 3 sts at beg of next 2 rows, 2 sts at beg of next 2 rows. **Next (dec) row (RS)** K2, k2tog, work to last 4 sts, ssk, k2. Rep dec row every other row 0 (0, 1, 1, 2) times every 4th row 6 times, every other row 0 (1, 1, 2, 2) times. Bind off 2 sts at beg of next 2 rows, 3 sts at beg of next 2 rows. Bind off rem 18 (20, 22, 24, 26) sts.

FINISHING

Block pieces to measurements. Sew one shoulder seam.

Collar

With WS facing, pick up and k113 sts evenly around neck edge. **Next row (WS)** P1, work bias rib to last st, p1. Cont in bias rib, working first and last sts in St st, until collar measures 8"/20.5cm. Bind off. Sew 2nd shoulder and collar seam.

Set in sleeves. Sew side and sleeve seams.

(Schematics on page 121)

Weather the Cold

For a little style, try these coats on for size.

Swing Kid

for intermediate knitters

Kathleen Power Johnson resurrects the A-line swing coat with this beautifully textured linen-stitch design. With no buttons and matching foldback lapels and cuffs, this easy beauty can turn any look into a clean, streamlined outfit. "Swing Kid" first appeared in the Fall '98 issue of *Family Circle Easy Knitting*.

MATERIALS

- *Lamb's Pride Bulky* by Brown Sheep Yarn Co., 4oz/113g skeins, each approx 125yd/114m (wool/mohair)
  10 (12, 14, 16, 18) skeins in #M-75 blue
- One pair size 13 (9mm) needles OR SIZE TO OBTAIN GAUGE
- Stitch holders

SIZES

Sized for Woman's Large (X-Large, 1X, 2X, 3X). Shown in size Large.

FINISHED MEASUREMENTS

- Bust (closed) 50 (52, 54½, 58, 62)"/127 (132, 138, 147, 157.5)cm
- Length 33 (33, 33½, 33½, 34)"/84 (84, 85, 85, 86.5)cm
- Upper arm 23¼ (23¼, 24¼, 24¼, 25)"/59 (59, 61.5, 61.5, 63.5)cm

GAUGE

23 sts and 36 rows to 6"/15.25cm over linen pat st using size 13 (9mm) needles.
TAKE TIME TO CHECK YOUR GAUGE.

LINEN PATTERN STITCH

(over an odd number of sts)
Row 1 (RS) K1, *sl 1 wyif, k1; rep from * to end.
Row 2 K1, p1, *sl 1 wyib, p1; rep from *, end k1.
Rep rows 1 and 2 for linen pat st.

BACK

Cast on 111 (115, 121, 127, 135) sts. Work in linen pat st, dec 1 st each side (inside selvage sts) every 16th row 4 times, then every 14th row 4 times—95 (99, 105, 111, 119) sts. Work even until piece measures 22"/56cm from beg.

Armhole shaping

Bind off 6 (6, 6, 6, 7) sts at beg of next 2 rows, 3 (3, 4, 4, 4) sts at beg of next 2 rows, then dec 1 st each side every 4th row 4 (4, 4, 5, 6) times. Work even on 69 (73, 77, 81, 85) sts until armhole measures 11 (11, 11½, 11½, 12)"/28 (28, 29, 29, 30.5)cm, end with a RS row.

Neck and shoulders

On next (WS) row, work 19 (21, 22, 24, 26) sts and place on a holder, bind off center 31 (31, 31, 33, 33) sts for neck, place rem sts on a holder.

LEFT FRONT

Cast on 73 (75, 79, 81, 85) sts. Work in linen pat st, dec 1 st at beg of RS rows (seam edge) every 16th row 4 times, then every 14th row 4 times—65 (67, 71, 73, 77) sts. Work even until piece measures 22"/56 cm from beg.

Armhole shaping

From armhole edge (beg of RS rows), bind off 6 (6, 6, 6, 7) sts once, 3 (3, 4, 4, 4) sts once, then dec 1 st every 4th row 4 (4, 4, 5, 6) times and AT SAME TIME, when armhole measures 1½"/4cm, beg neck shaping as foll:

Neck shaping

Next row (RS) Work pat to last 3 sts, k2tog, k1. Cont to dec 1 st at neck edge (inside selvage st) every 6th row 5 (5, 1, 3, 3) times, every 4th row 5 (5, 11, 8, 8) times—41 (43, 44, 46, 48) sts rem. Work even until same length as back armhole. **Next row (RS)** Work 19 (21, 22, 24, 26) sts and place on a holder for shoulder, M1 inc st, then work rem 22 sts for lapel. Cont to work on lapel sts with M1 inc at inside edge every 6th row once then every 4th row 4 times—28 sts. Work even until lapel fits to center of back neck. Leave sts on a holder.

RIGHT FRONT

Work as for left front, reversing all shaping.

SLEEVES

Cast on 41 (41, 43, 43, 45) sts. Work in linen pat st for 3"/7.5cm, dec 4 sts evenly across last WS row (foldline)—37 (37, 39, 39, 41) sts. Cont in pat, inc 1 st each side (inside selvage sts) every 4th row 22 times, every 2nd row 4 (4, 5, 5, 5) times—89 (89, 93, 93, 95) sts. Work even until piece measures 20"/50.5cm from beg.

Cap shaping

Bind off 6 sts at beg of next 2 rows, 4 sts at beg of next 6 rows, 2 sts at beg of next 18 rows. Bind off rem 17 (17, 21, 21, 23) sts.

FINISHING

Block pieces to measurements. Knit tog shoulder seams and back collar seam. Sew collar to back neck so that seam is on RS of garment (this is WS of collar). Sew sleeves into armholes. Sew side seams. Sew sleeve seams with last 3"/7.5cm seam on RS for cuff turnback.

(Schematics on page 122)

Swirl of Gold

Fashion-forward doesn't have to be synonymous with discomfort, as this stockinette-stitched cropped jacket shows. The design's centerpiece is a swirling one-button closure that's enhanced by ribbed cuffs and neckline. "Swirl of Gold" first appeared in the Winter '98/'99 issue of *Family Circle Easy Knitting*.

MATERIALS
- *Puffy* by Karabella Yarns, 3¹⁄₂oz/100g balls, each approx 54yd/47m (wool)
  9 (10, 11) balls in #52 gold
- One pair size 11 (8mm) needles OR SIZE TO OBTAIN GAUGE
- One set size 9 (5.5mm) dpn
- One 1¹⁄₂"/38mm button

SIZES
Sized for Small (Medium, Large). Shown in size Medium.

FINISHED MEASUREMENTS
- Bust (closed) 42 (44, 47)"/106.5 (111.5, 119)cm
- Length 18¹⁄₂ (19, 19¹⁄₂)"/47 (48.5, 49.5)cm
- Upper arm 15 (16, 17)"/38 (40.5, 43)cm

GAUGE
9 sts and 13 rows to 4"/10cm over St st using size 11 (8mm) needles.
TAKE TIME TO CHECK YOUR GAUGE.

BACK
Cast on 46 (50, 52) sts. Work in k1, p1 rib for 1"/2.5cm, inc 1 (0, 1) on last WS row—47 (50, 53) sts. Work even in St st until piece measures 17¹⁄₂ (18, 18¹⁄₂)"/44.5 (45.5, 47)cm from beg.

Neck shaping
Next row (RS) Work 18 (19, 20) sts, join a 2nd ball of yarn and bind off center 11 (12, 13) sts, work to end. Working both sides at once with separate balls of yarn, dec 1 st from each neck edge every other row once. When piece measures 18¹⁄₂ (19, 19¹⁄₂)"/47 (48.5, 49.5)cm from beg, bind off rem 17 (18, 19) sts each side for shoulders.

LEFT FRONT
Cast on 25 (27, 29) sts. Work in k1, p1 rib for 1"/2.5cm. **Next row (RS)** K21 (23, 25) sts, [p1, k1] twice (for front band). Cont as established, with last 4 sts in rib for front band, until piece measures 15¹⁄₂ (16, 16¹⁄₂)"/39.5 (40.5, 42)cm from beg, end with a RS row.

Neck shaping
Next row (WS) Bind off 4 sts (neck edge), work to end. Cont to bind off from neck edge 2 sts twice, 1 st 0 (1, 2) times—17 (18, 19) sts. When same length as back, bind off rem sts for shoulders.

RIGHT FRONT
Work to correspond to left front, reversing shaping.

SLEEVES
Cast on 22 (24, 24) sts. Work in k1, p1 rib for 1"/2.5cm. Cont in St st, inc 1 st each side every 8th (8th, 6th) row 6 (6, 7) times—34 (36, 38) sts. Work even until piece measures 16"/40.5cm from beg. Bind off.

FINISHING
Block pieces to measurements. Sew shoulder seams. Pick up and k 41 (43, 45) sts evenly around neck and work in k1, p1 rib for 1"/2.5cm. Bind off in rib. Place markers 7¹⁄₂ (8, 8¹⁄₂)"/19 (20.5, 21.5)cm down from shoulders on front and back. Sew top of sleeves between markers. Sew side and sleeve seams.

Frog
(I-cord)
With 2 dpn, cast on 3 sts. K3. Sl sts to other end of needle and bring yarn around to k the 3 sts (from RS) again. Cont in this way to form I-cord until piece measures 17"/43cm from beg. Curl cord into shape as shown in photo, with loop for button, and sew to form figure eight shape. Sew curled end of frog to right front at 3"/7.5cm from top edge. Sew on button opposite loop.

(Schematics on page 122)

Red All Over

for intermediate knitters

Soft, graceful and oh-so-smart, this Betsy Westman machine-knit design uses a mohair/wool blend to create lots of warmth, but little bulk. A plunging neckline and button closure are splendid details deserving of such a chic coat. "Red All Over" first appeared in the Winter '01/'02 issue of *Family Circle Easy Knitting*.

MATERIALS

- *La Gran* by Classic Elite Yarns, 1¹⁄₂oz/42g balls, each approx 90yd/81m (mohair/wool)
  15 (15, 16, 17, 18) balls in #6527 red
- One pair size 9 (5.5 mm) needles (for handknitting) OR SIZE TO OBTAIN GAUGE
- #3¹⁄₂ keyplate (for machine knitting)
- One 1"/2.5cm button

SIZES

Sized for Medium, (Large, X-Large, 1X, 2X). Shown in size Large.

FINISHED MEASUREMENTS

- Lower edge 49 (52, 55, 58, 61)"/124 (132, 140, 147, 155)cm
- Bust 45 (48, 51, 54, 57)"/114 (122, 130, 137, 145)cm
- Length 35 (35¹⁄₂, 36, 36¹⁄₂, 37)"/89 (90, 91.5, 93, 94)cm
- Upper arm 15 (16, 17, 18, 19)"/38.5, 41, 43.5, 46, 48.5)cm

GAUGE

- 16 sts and 23 rows to 4"/10cm over St st using #3¹⁄₂ keyplate (machine knit).
- 16 sts and 20 rows to 4"/10cm over St st using size 9 (5.5mm) needles (handknit).

TAKE TIME TO CHECK YOUR GAUGE.

ABBREVIATIONS

(for machine knit)
WY waste yarn
COL carriage on left
COR carriage on right

Notes

1 Numbers for handknitting are in italics following numbers for machine knitting. If there is only one set of numbers, it applies to both machine and hand knitting.

2 Row counts are for machine knitting only. Inches/cm are given, when needed, for handknitting.

3 Note that cast-on sts apply to both methods. Handknitting instructions beg "Join MC".

4 Do not bind off handknitting before reading all instructions in each section.

LEFT BACK

With WY cast on 58 (60, 64, 66, 70) sts using the open edge cast-on method and work 6 rows. Break off WY. *Join MC* and work 63 (66, 68, 71, 74) rows, *12¹⁄₂ (13, 13¹⁄₂, 14, 14¹⁄₂)"/31.5 (33, 34, 35.5, 37)cm* St st. Dec 1 st at side on next row and every 17 (15 for hand) rows 3 times more—54 (56, 60, 62, 66) sts and 115 (118, 120, 123, 126) rows. Work even to 129 (133, 135, 137, 141) rows, *26¹⁄₂"/67cm*, complete ending with a COL.

Armhole shaping

Bind off 4 sts at beg of next row. Work 1 row even. Dec 1 st at side edge every other row 5 (5, 5, 6, 7) times—45 (47, 51, 52, 55) sts. Work even to 184 (188, 190, 196, 210) rows, *35 (35¹⁄₂, 36, 36¹⁄₂, 37)"/89 (90, 91.5, 93, 94)cm*, ending with a COR. Push needles to holding position and place the green cards to hold them. Bind off (machine knit only) with tapestry needle using back st method. Remove work from machine. Remove WY from lower edge and pick up sts with needles. With MC and hand knitting needles, work 6 rows seed st ending with a WS row. Bind off. Place marker 13"/33 cm from lower edge on center back. With needles, pick up and k 52 sts between lower edge and marker. Work 4 rows seed st, and bind off for vent.

RIGHT BACK

Work to correspond to left back reversing all shaping.

LEFT FRONT

Work as for left back until shaping is completed— 54 (56, 60, 62, 66) sts and *115 (118, 120, 123, 126) rows, 22 (22¹⁄₂, 23, 23¹⁄₂, 24)"/56 (57, 58.5, 59.5, 61)cm*.

Neck shaping

Dec 1 st neck edge every other row 10 times and every 3rd row 16 times, AT SAME TIME work armhole shaping when there are 129 (133, 135, 137, 141) rows (*same as back to armhole*), complete ending with COL. Bind off 4 sts at beg of next row. Work 1 row. Bind off 1 st at side edge every other row 5 (5, 5, 6, 7) times. Work even until 184 (188, 190, 196, 210) rows are completed and 19 (21, 25, 26, 29) sts (*and same length as back*). Bind off (machine knit only) as for left back. Remove WY from lower edge and pick up sts with needles. With MC

(Continued on page 123)

Pattern Play

for intermediate knitters

Employ a classic technique to create the stunning two-tone mosaic pattern of this snazzy serape. Combining both stockinette and garter stitch in contrasting colors, this deceptively easy-to-knit design by Barbara Venishnick works up in a flash with big needles and chunky yarn. "Pattern Play" first appeared in the Holiday '03 issue of *Family Circle Easy Knitting*.

MATERIALS
■ *Up Country* by Patons®, 3½oz/100g balls, each approx 78yd/70m (wool)
   8 (8) balls in #80930 khaki (MC)
   9 (9) balls in #80906 cream (CC)
■ One pair size 15 (10mm) circular needles 29"/74cm long OR SIZE TO OBTAIN GAUGE
■ Size I/9 (5.5mm) crochet hook

SIZES
Sized for one size.

FINISHED MEASUREMENTS
■ 47"/119cm wide by 32"/81cm long

GAUGE
10½ sts and 17¼ rows to 4"/10cm over reverse St st using size 10 (6mm) needles.
TAKE TIME TO CHECK YOUR GAUGE.

Notes
1 One row of chart represents two rows of knitting.

2 Work first row of chart (2 rows of knitting) with B, then cont to alternate 2 rows each A and B.

3 Work A sts in St st and B sts in garter st.

SERAPE
With A, cast on 125 sts. Foll chart, work first st of chart, work 10-st rep 12 times, work last 4 sts of chart. Cont in this way to rep rows 1-16 until piece measures 32"/81cm from beg, end with a WS row.

Divide for neck opening and fronts
Note Pm at beg and end of row. Work 55 sts, join a 2nd ball of yarn and bind off center 15 sts, work to end. Working both sides at once, cont in chart as established until piece measures same as back, end with a RS row color A.
Next row (WS) Bind off knitwise with A.

FINISHING
With RS facing, crochet hook and A, work sc in each color A row along outer right side edge (skip all B rows). Rep on outer left side edge. Rep on inner right edge, work 1 sc in each bound-off st on back neck, work down inner left edge as for right side.
For armholes, measure 14"/35.5cm from markers down front and tack in place with back.

(Schematics on page 123)

Turning Leaves

Celebrate fall in this Nicky Epstein design that literally knits the colors of the season into the sweater. Knitted appliqué leaves adorn the lapels and pockets of this fine garter-stitch cardigan coat. "Turning Leaves" first appeared in the Fall '99 issue of *Family Circle Easy Knitting*.

MATERIALS

- *Allagash* by Reynolds/JCA, 3¹/₂oz/100g balls, each approx 93yd/84m (wool/nylon) 16 (17, 18, 19) balls in #647 burgundy (MC)
- *Fusion* by Reynolds/JCA, 1³/₄oz/50g balls each approx 136yd/121m (wool) 1 ball each in #11 blue (A), #5 red multi (B) and #9 brown multi (C)
- One pair size 10¹/₂ (7mm) needles OR SIZE TO OBTAIN GAUGE
- One set (4) size 5 (3.75mm) dpn
- Stitch holders
- Three 1"/25mm buttons

SIZES

Sized for Medium (Large, X-Large, XX-Large). Shown in size XX-Large.

FINISHED MEASUREMENTS

- Bust (closed) 51 (53, 55, 58)"/129.5 (134.5, 139.5, 147)cm
- Length 29³/₄ (30¹/₄, 31¹/₄, 32¹/₂)"/75.5 (76.5, 79.5, 82.5)cm
- Upper arm 17¹/₂ (18, 18, 19¹/₂)"/44.5 (45.5, 45.5, 49.5)cm

GAUGE

11 sts and 21 rows to 4"/10cm over garter st using MC and size 10¹/₂ (7mm) needles. TAKE TIME TO CHECK YOUR GAUGE.

BACK

With MC, cast on 66 (69, 72, 76) sts. Work in garter st until piece measures 18¹/₂ (19, 20, 20)"/47 (48, 51, 51)cm from beg.

Raglan armhole shaping

Bind off 2 (3, 3, 3) sts at beg of next 2 rows—62 (63, 66, 70) sts. ***Dec row 1** K1, k2tog, k to last 3 sts, ssk, k1. Work 1 row even. **Next row** Rep dec row 1. Work 3 rows even.* Rep between *'s 8 (8, 8, 9) times more—26 (27, 30, 30) sts. Bind off.

Pocket lining

With size 10¹/₂ (7mm) needles and MC, cast on 20 sts. Work in St st for 7"/18cm. Place sts on a holder.

LEFT FRONT

With MC, cast on 41 (43, 44, 46) sts. Work in garter st until piece measures 10"/25.5cm from beg. **Next row (RS)** K8 (9, 9, 10), bind off next 20 sts (for pocket), k to end. **Next row** K13 (14, 15, 16), k 20 sts of pocket lining from holder, k to end. Work even on all sts until piece measures 18¹/₂ (19, 20, 20)"/47 (48, 51, 51)cm from beg, end with a WS row.

Raglan armhole shaping

Bind off 2 (3, 3, 3) sts at beg of next row—39 (40, 41, 43) sts. Then work raglan armhole dec at beg of RS rows only as for back—21 (22, 23, 23) sts rem. Place these sts on a holder.

RIGHT FRONT

Work as for left front, reversing placement of pocket at 13 (14, 15, 16) sts from center edge and forming 5 buttonholes, the first one at 9¹/₂ (10, 11, 11)"/24 (25, 28, 28)cm from lower edge, the other 2 spaced at 4"/10cm intervals as foll: **Buttonhole row (RS)** K3, bind off 3 sts k to end. **Next row** K, casting on 3 sts over bound-off sts of previous row. Cont as for left front reversing armhole shaping by working at end of RS rows.

SLEEVES

With 34 (34, 36, 36) sts. Work in garter st for 6"/15.5cm (end of cuff). Inc 1 st each side of next row then every 4th row 6 (7, 6, 8) times more—48 (50, 50, 54) sts. Work even until piece measures 19 (19¹/₂, 19¹/₂, 18¹/₂)"/48 (49.5, 49.5, 47)cm from beg.

Raglan cap shaping

Work as for raglan armhole shaping on back—8 sts rem. Bind off.

FINISHING

Block pieces to measurements. Sew raglan caps into raglan armholes.

Collar

With MC, work across 21 (22, 23, 23) sts from left front holder and work in garter st for 7¹/₂ (8, 8¹/₂, 8¹/₂)"/19 (20.5, 21.5, 21.5)cm or until collar fits to center back neck. Bind off. Work collar on right front in same way. Sew collar tog at center back. Sew collar to neck edge. Sew pocket linings in place. Sew 6"/15.5cm of

(Continued on page 124)

Toggles with a Twist

for intermediate knitters

The toggle coat is a favorite among New England preppies, but this new knitted version takes it from functional to fashionable. A broad collar brings finesse to the no-nonsense design and double-strand knitting with two colors makes for a multidimensional stockinette stitch. "Toggles with a Twist" first appeared in the Winter '00/'01 issue of *Family Circle Easy Knitting*.

MATERIALS

- *14 Ply* by Wool Pak Yarns NZ/ Baabajoes Wool Co., 8¹/₂oz/250g balls, each approx 310yd/286m (wool)

  7 (7, 8, 8) balls each in charcoal (A) and sand (B)
- One pair size 15 (10mm) needles OR SIZE TO OBTAIN GAUGE
- Six toggle buttons

SIZES

Sized for Medium (Large, X-Large, XX-Large). Shown in size Large.

FINISHED MEASUREMENTS

- Bust (buttoned) 44 (47, 50, 53)"/111.5 (119, 127, 134.5)cm
- Length 29 (30, 30¹/₂, 31¹/₂)"/73.5 (76.5, 77.5, 80)cm
- Upper arm 20 (21, 21¹/₂, 22¹/₂)"/50.5 (53.5, 54.5, 57)cm

GAUGE

10 sts and 14 rows to 4"/10cm over St st using size 15 (10mm) needles and 1 strand each A and B held tog.
TAKE TIME TO CHECK YOUR GAUGE.

BACK

With 1 strand each A and B held tog, cast on 54 (58, 62, 66) sts. K 1 row on WS, then work in St st until piece measures 18¹/₂ (19, 19, 19¹/₂)"/47 (48.5, 48.5, 49.5)cm from beg.

Armhole shaping

Bind off 2 sts at beg of next 4 rows—46 (50, 54, 58) sts. Work even until armhole measures 9¹/₂ (10, 10¹/₂, 11)"/24 (25.5, 26.5, 28)cm.

Shoulder and neck shaping

Bind off 8 (8, 9, 10) sts at beg of next 2 rows, 8 (9, 10, 10) sts at beg of next 2 rows, AT SAME TIME, bind off center 10 (12, 12, 14) sts for neck and working both sides at once, bind off 2 sts from each neck edge once.

LEFT FRONT

With 1 strand each A and B held tog, cast on 30 (32, 34, 36) sts. K 1 row on WS. **Next row (RS)** Work in St st over 27 (29, 31, 33) sts, work rev St st over next 2 sts, work last st in garter st. Cont in pats as established until same length as back to armhole. Shape armhole at side edge (beg of RS rows) as for back—26 (28, 30, 32) sts. Work even until armhole measures 7¹/₂ (8, 8¹/₂, 9)"/19 (20.5, 21.5, 23)cm, end with a RS row.

Neck and shoulder shaping

Next row (WS) Bind off 5 (6, 6, 7) sts (neck edge), work to end. Cont to bind off from neck edge 2 sts once, 1 st 3 times, AT SAME TIME, when same length as back to shoulder, shape shoulder at side edge as for back. Place markers on front band for 6 buttons, with the first on ¹/₄"/1cm below neck shaping, the last on 8"/20.5cm from lower edge, and 4 others spaced evenly between.

RIGHT FRONT

Work to correspond to left front, reversing all shaping and pats as foll: K 1 row on WS. **Next row (RS)** Work 1 st in garter st, 2 sts in rev St st, work rem sts in St st. Work buttonhole in front band opposite markers as foll: **Next row (RS)** Work 2 sts, yo, k2tog, work to end.

SLEEVES

With 1 strand each A and B held tog, cast on 24 (26, 26, 28) sts. K 1 row on WS, then work in St st, inc 1 st each side every 4th row 13 (13, 14, 14) times—50 (52, 54, 56) sts. Work even until piece measures 17 (17¹/₂, 17¹/₂, 18)"/43 (44.5, 44.5, 45.5)cm from beg.

Cap shaping

Dec 1 st each side on next row, then every other row twice more. Bind off rem 44 (46, 48, 50) sts.

FINISHING

Block pieces to measurements. Sew shoulder seams.

Collar

With RS facing, pick up and k 48 (52, 52, 56) sts evenly around neck edge. **Next row (WS)** Work 1 st in garter st, 2 sts in rev St st, 42 (46, 46, 50) sts in St st, 2 sts in rev St st, 1 st in garter st. Cont as established until collar measures 23/4"/7cm, end with a WS row. **Next row (RS)** Work 9 sts, [M1, work 6 (7, 7, 8) sts] 5 times, M1, work 9 (8, 8, 7) sts—54 (58, 58, 62) sts. Work 2"/5cm even. Inc 5 sts evenly spaced across next row—59 (63, 63, 67) sts. Work even until collar measures 8"/20.5cm, end with a RS row. K 1 row on WS, then bind off loosely. Set in sleeves. Sew side and sleeve seams. Sew on buttons.

(Schematics on page 124)

City Chic

A simple belted coat can add panache to any outfit in seconds flat! This Joanne Yordanou design mixes it up with seed-stitch details and both traditional and reverse stockinette stitches. Work in a low-cut neckline and turn back the sleeves and you're ready to hit the street. "City Chic" first appeared in the Fall '02 issue of *Family Circle Easy Knitting*.

MATERIALS

■ *Gusto 10* by Cleckheaton/Plymouth Yarns, 3½oz/100g balls, each approx 56yd/51m (acrylic/wool/mohair)
22 (24, 25, 26) balls in #2095 blue
■ One pair size 13 (9mm) needles OR SIZE TO OBTAIN GAUGE
■ Size K/10½ (7mm) crochet hook
■ Seven 1¼"/32mm buttons

SIZES

Sized for Medium (Large, X-Large, XX-Large). Shown in size X-Large.

FINISHED MEASUREMENTS

■ Bust (buttoned) 47 (49, 52½, 57½)"/119 (124.5, 133, 146)cm
■ Length 39½ (39½, 40, 40)"/100 (100, 101.5, 101.5)cm
■ Upper arm 19 (19, 20, 20)"/48 (48, 51, 51)cm

GAUGE

9 sts and 12 rows to 4"/10cm over St st using size 13 (9mm) needles.
TAKE TIME TO CHECK YOUR GAUGE.

SEED STITCH

Row 1 (RS) *K1, p1; rep from * to end.
Row 2 K the purl sts and p the knit sts.
Rep row 2 for seed st.

BACK

Cast on 47 (49, 53, 57) sts. Work in seed st for 4"/10cm, inc 6 (6, 6, 8) sts evenly across last WS row—53 (55, 59, 65) sts. Work in reverse St st until piece measures 28"/71cm from beg.

Armhole shaping

Bind off 3 (3, 4, 4) sts at beg of next 2 rows—47 (49, 51, 57) sts. Work even until armhole measures 9½ (9½, 10, 10)"/24 (24, 25.5, 25.5)cm.

Shoulder shaping

Bind off 5 (5, 5, 6) sts at beg of next 4 rows, 5 (6, 6, 7) sts at beg of next 2 rows. Bind off 17 (17, 19, 19) sts for back neck.

LEFT FRONT

Cast on 23 (25, 27, 29) sts. Work in seed st for 4"/10cm, inc 2 sts evenly across last WS row—25 (27, 29, 31) sts. Work in reverse St st until piece measures 24"/61cm from beg, end with a WS row. **Next row (RS)** P to last st, k1. **Next row (WS)** P2, k to end. Cont as established, working 1 more st as St st on every row until all sts are St st, AT SAME TIME, when piece measures same as back to armhole, work armhole and neck shaping as foll:

Armhole and neck shaping

Next row (RS) Bind off 3 (3, 4, 4) sts, work to last 2 sts, k2tog. Dec 1 st at neck edge every other row 6 (7, 8, 7) times more—15 (16, 16, 19) sts. Work even until piece measures same as back to shoulder, shape shoulder as on back.

RIGHT FRONT

Work to correspond to left front, reversing all shaping.

SLEEVES

Cast on 25 (25, 27, 27) sts. Work in seed st for 4"/10cm. Work in reverse St st, AT SAME TIME, inc 1 st each side of next row, then every 4th row 3 (3, 2, 1) times, every 6th row 5 (5, 6, 7) times—43 (43, 45, 45) sts. Work even until piece measures 19 (20, 21, 22)"/50 (52, 53.5, 56)cm from beg. Bind off loosely.

FINISHING

Block pieces to measurements. Sew shoulder seams

Pocket

Cast on 17 sts. Work in seed st for 8"/20.5cm. Bind off in seed st. Place pocket on right front, 9"/23cm (or length as desired) from lower edge. Sew in place.

Belt

Cast on 5 sts. Work in seed st for 50"/127cm. Bind off in seed st.

Belt loops

(make 2)
With crochet hook, ch 7. Fasten off, leaving long end for attaching. Mark desired position of belt loops and sew in place.

Collar

With RS facing, pick up and k61 (61, 63, 63) sts around neck edge. Work in seed st for 6"/15cm. Bind off in seed st.

Front bands

Pick up and k69 sts along left front to neck

(Continued on page 125)

So Simple

"Less is more" is an adage that certainly applies to this cardigan design from Loren Cherensky, shown here in two different colors. Clean lines and easy styling with garter-stitched detail shows how marvelous simplicity can be. "So Simple" first appeared in the Fall '01 issue of *Family Circle Easy Knitting*.

MATERIALS

■ *Lamb's Pride Bulky* by Brown Sheep Yarn Co., 4oz/125g balls, each approx 125yd/115m (wool/mohair)
23 (24, 25, 26, 27) balls in #M113 olive or #M150 navy
■ One pair size 15 (10mm) needles OR SIZE TO OBTAIN GAUGE
■ Five 1¼"/32mm buttons
■ Stitch holders

SIZES

Sized for Small (Medium, Large, X-Large, XX-Large). Shown in size Large.

FINISHED MEASUREMENTS

■ Bust (buttoned) 46 (48, 50, 53, 56)"/117 (122, 127, 134.5, 142)cm
■ Length 31 (31, 31½, 32, 32½)"/78.5 (78.5, 80, 81, 82.5)cm
■ Upper arm 16¾ (16¾, 17½, 18½, 19¼)"/42.5 (42.5, 44.5, 47, 49)cm

GAUGE

10 sts and 15 rows to 4"/10cm over St st using size 15 (10mm) needles.
TAKE TIME TO CHECK YOUR GAUGE.

BACK

Cast on 58 (60, 62, 66, 70) sts. Work in garter st for 6 rows. Then, cont in St st until piece measures 22"/56cm from beg.

Armhole shaping

Bind off 5 sts at beg of next 2 rows. Dec 1 st each side every other row 6 (6, 6, 7, 8) times—36 (38, 40, 42, 44) sts. Work even until armhole measures 8 (8, 8½, 9, 9½)"/20.5 (20.5, 21.5, 23, 24)cm.

Neck and shoulder shaping

Bind off 5 (7, 7, 7, 7) sts at beg of next 2 rows, 6 (5, 5, 6, 7) sts at beg of next 2 rows. Bind off rem 14 (14, 16, 16, 16) sts for back neck.

POCKET LINING

(make 2)
Cast on 18 sts. Work in St st for 6"/15cm, end with a p row. Sl sts to a holder.

LEFT FRONT

Cast on 36 (37, 38, 40, 42) sts. Work in garter st for 6 rows. **Next row (RS)** Knit. **Next row** K6 (front border) p to end. Rep last 2 rows until piece measures 10"/25.5cm from beg, end with a RS row.

Pocket opening

Next row (WS) Work 13 (14, 14, 15, 16) sts, p18 and sl these sts to a holder for pocket border, p to end. **Next row** K5 (5, 6, 7, 8), k18 sts of pocket lining, k to end. Cont on all sts until piece measures 22"/56cm from beg, end with a WS row.

Armhole shaping

Bind off 5 sts at beg of next row (armhole edge). Cont to dec 1 st at armhole edge every other row 6 (6, 6, 7, 8) times—25 (26, 27, 28, 29) sts. Work even until armhole measures 5½ (5½, 6, 6½, 7)"/14 (14, 15, 16.5, 18)cm.

Neck shaping

Next row (WS) Bind off 6 sts, work to end. Cont to shape neck, binding off 2 sts every other row 4 times, dec 1 st every other row 0 (0, 1, 1, 1) time, AT SAME TIME, shape shoulder when same length as back. Place markers for 5 buttons evenly spaced, the first one at 1½"/4cm from lower edge, the top one at 1"/2.5cm from top edge and the others evenly spaced.

RIGHT FRONT

Work to correspond to left front, reversing shaping and pocket placement and working buttonholes opposite markers as foll: **Buttonhole row (RS)** K3, yo, k2tog, work to end.

SLEEVES

Cast on 26 (26, 28, 28, 30) sts. Work in garter st for 6 rows. Then, cont in St st inc 1 st each side every 6th row 5 (5, 5, 9, 9) times, every 8th row 3 (3, 3, 0, 0) times—42 (42, 44, 46, 48) sts. Work even until piece measures 16½ (16½, 16½, 17, 17)"/42 (42, 42, 43, 43)cm from beg.

Cap shaping

Bind off 5 sts at beg of next 2 rows. Dec 1 st each side every other row 9 (9, 10, 11, 12) times. Bind off 2 sts at beg of next 2 rows. Bind off rem 10 sts.

FINISHING

Block pieces to measurements.

Pocket border

Work across 18 sts from one pocket holder and k6 rows. Bind off. Sew shoulder seams.

Collar

Pick up and k 56 (56, 60, 60, 60) sts evenly around neck edge. Work in garter st for 4"/10cm. Bind off. Sew sleeves into armholes.

(Schematics on page 125)

On the Bias

for beginner knitters

Who said that you shouldn't wear stripes? Texture and understated stripes coexist brilliantly in this slimming V-neck coat from designer Norah Gaughan. The diagonal pattern creates a bias effect, with a single-button closure just under the neckline for easy on and easy off. "On the Bias" first appeared in the Fall '00 issue of *Family Circle Easy Knitting*.

MATERIALS

- *Harmony* by Reynolds/JCA, 4oz/125g hanks each approx 173yd/159m (wool)
  10 (10, 11, 12, 13) hanks in #015 rust multi
- One pair size 8 (5mm) needles OR SIZE TO OBTAIN GAUGE
- One 1¹/₂"/38mm toggle

SIZES

Sized for Large (X-Large, 1X, 2X, 3X). Shown in size X-Large.

FINISHED MEASUREMENTS

- Bust 48 (51, 54, 60, 63)"/122 (129.5, 137, 152, 160)cm
- Length 29¹/₂ (30, 30¹/₂, 31, 31¹/₂)"/75 (76, 77.5, 78.5, 80)cm
- Upper arm 19 (20, 21, 22, 23)"/48 (51, 53, 56, 58)cm

GAUGE

16 sts and 24 rows to 4"/10cm over chart pat using size 8 (5mm) needles.
TAKE TIME TO CHECK YOUR GAUGE.

Note

For best results for staggering of color pat, alternate between 2 balls of yarn, switching balls every 2 rows.

BACK

Cast on 96 (102, 108, 120, 126) sts. Work 6-st rep of chart pat until piece measures 29¹/₂ (30, 30¹/₂, 31, 31¹/₂)"/75 (76, 77.5, 78.5, 80)cm from beg. Bind off.

RIGHT FRONT, COLLAR AND LEFT FRONT

Beg at lower right front edge, cast on 60 (63, 66, 72, 75) sts. Beg with st 4 (1, 4, 4, 1) of chart, work 6-st rep until piece measures 29¹/₂ (30, 30¹/₂, 31, 31¹/₂)"/75 (76, 77.5, 78.5, 80)cm from beg, end with a RS row. **Next row (WS)** Bind off 27 (30, 33, 39, 42) sts for shoulder, work to end. Cont on 33 sts for collar for 10"/25.5cm, end with a RS row. **Next row (WS)** Cast on 27 (30, 33, 39, 42) sts for left front shoulder, work to end. Cont in pat as established until left front measures 10"/25.5cm. **Next row (WS)** Work 10 sts, bind off 3 sts for buttonhole, work to end. Cast on 38 sts over bound-off sts on next row. Cont in pat until same length as right front. Bind off.

SLEEVES

Cast on 48 (54, 54, 60, 60) sts. Work 6-st rep of chart pat until piece measures 6"/15cm from beg. Inc 1 st each side of next row, then every 6th row 4 (0, 7, 4, 11) times more, every 8th row 9 (12, 7, 9, 4) times—76 (80, 84, 88, 92) sts. Work even until piece measures 23"/58.5cm from beg. Bind off.

POCKETS

Cast on 24 sts. Work 6-st rep of chart pat for 6"/15cm. Bind off.

FINISHING

Block pieces to measurements. Sew shoulder seams. Sew collar across back neck. Place markers at 9¹/₂ (10, 10¹/₂, 11, 11¹/₂)"/24 (25.5, 26.5, 28, 29)cm down from shoulders. Sew sleeves to armholes between markers. Sew side and sleeve seams. Turn up sleeve cuffs for 4"/10cm and tack down at seam. Sew on pockets. Sew on button.

(Schematics on page 126)

Warm Front

This sporty zippered jacket is just right for an active but arctic weekend. Reverse stockinette stitch is anything but ordinary, and a rolled neckband is a youthful twist on the typical collar. The self-patterning yarn means that you get all of the color without any of the effort. "Warm Front" first appeared in the Fall '03 issue of *Family Circle Easy Knitting*.

MATERIALS

- *Fantastica* by GGH/Muench Yarns, 1¾oz/50g balls, each approx 30yd/28m (wool/acrylic/alpaca/nylon)
  20 (21, 22, 24, 25) balls in #04 brown multi
- One pair size 17 (12.75mm) needles OR SIZE TO OBTAIN GAUGE
- One separating zipper 20 (20, 20, 22, 22)"/50 (50, 50, 55, 55)cm long
- Stitch holders

SIZES

Sized for Small (Medium, Large, X-Large, XX-Large). Shown in size Medium.

FINISHED MEASUREMENTS

- Bust (closed) 40 (42, 46, 48, 52)"/101.5 (106.5, 117, 122, 132)cm
- Length 22 (22½, 22½, 24, 24½)"/56 (57.5, 57.5, 61, 62.5)cm
- Upper arm 17 (18, 19, 19, 20)"/43 (46, 48, 48, 51)cm

GAUGE

8 sts and 11 rows to 4"/10cm over reverse St st using size 17 (12.75mm) needles.
TAKE TIME TO CHECK YOUR GAUGE.

BACK

Cast on 41 (43, 47, 49, 53) sts. Work in reverse St st for 13½ (13½, 13½, 14½, 14½)"/34.5 (34.5, 34.5, 37, 37)cm.

Armhole shaping

Bind off 4 (4, 5, 5, 6) sts at beg of next 2 rows—33 (35, 37, 39, 41) sts. Work even until armhole measures 8½ (9, 9½, 9½, 10)"/21.5 (23, 24, 24, 25.5)cm. Bind off all sts.

LEFT FRONT

Cast on 21 (22, 24, 25, 27) sts.

Next row (RS) Work in reverse St st to last 2 sts, work last 2 sts in St st (front edge). Cont as established until same length as back to armholes. Shape armhole at side edge (beg of RS row) as for back—17 (18, 19, 20, 21) sts. Work even until armhole measures 6½ (6½, 7, 7½, 7½)"/16.5 (16.5, 17.5, 19, 19)cm.

Neck shaping

Next row (RS) Work to last 5 (5, 5, 6, 6) sts and place them on a holder for neck. Cont to bind off from neck edge 2 sts once, 1 sts once. When same length as back, bind off rem 9 (10, 11, 11, 12) sts for shoulder.

RIGHT FRONT

Work to correspond to left front, reversing placement of St st front band (beg of RS rows) and all shaping.

SLEEVES

Cast on 21 sts. Work in reverse St st, inc 1 st each side every 4th row 0 (0, 2, 2, 5) times, every 6th row 7 (8, 7, 7, 5) times—35 (37, 39, 39, 41) sts. Work even until piece measures 19½ (20, 20½, 21, 21½)"/49.5 (50.5, 52 53.5, 54.5)cm from beg. Bind off all sts.

FINISHING

Block pieces to measurements. Sew shoulder seams.

Collar

With RS facing, pick up and k 44 (44, 44, 48, 48) sts evenly around neck edge, including sts from holders. Work in reverse St st, keeping 2 sts at front edges in St st, for 5"/13 cm. Bind off. Fold collar in half to WS and sew in place.
Set in sleeves, sewing last 2 (2, 2½, 2½, 3)"/5 (5, 6.5, 6.5, 7.5)cm at top of sleeve to bound-off armhole sts. Sew side and sleeve seams. Sew in zipper.

(Continued on page 126)

Fur Sure

for intermediate knitters

Fur is back in full force on the runway these days, and why should knitters be deprived of such a luxurious look? Heather Lodinsky's use of rich red yarn and lush cables topped with a ready-made faux fur collar make this style gorgeously glamorous. "Fur Sure" first appeared in the Winter '01/'02 issue of *Family Circle Easy Knitting*.

MATERIALS
- *Baby* by Tahki Yarns/Tahki•Stacy Charles, Inc., 3¹/₂oz/100g balls, each approx 60yd/55m (wool) 15 (17, 18, 20, 22, 23) balls in #20 red (MC)
- One pair each sizes 8 and 13 (5 and 9mm) needles OR SIZE TO OBTAIN GAUGE
- Size I/9 (5.5mm) crochet hook
- Ready-made faux fur collar (optional) *Softy* by Muench Yarns
- Cable needle
- 2 sets hooks and eyes

SIZES
Sized for X-Small (Small, Medium, Large, X-Large, XX-Large). Shown in size Medium.

FINISHED MEASUREMENTS
- Bust (closed) 39¹/₂ (41¹/₂, 47¹/₂, 49¹/₂, 55¹/₂, 57¹/₂)"/100 (105.5, 120.5, 125.5, 141, 146)cm
- Length 26 (27, 27, 27, 28, 28)"/66 (68.5, 68.5, 68.5, 71, 71)cm
- Upper arm 18 (20, 20, 20, 22, 22)"/45.5 (50.5, 50.5, 50.5, 56, 56)cm

GAUGE
12 sts and 16 rows to 4"/10cm over cable pat using size 13 (9mm) needles.
TAKE TIME TO CHECK YOUR GAUGE.

CABLE PATTERN
(multiple of 6 sts plus 2)
Row 1 (and all WS rows) Purl. **Row 2** Knit. **Row 4** K1, *k2, sl 2 to cn and hold to *back*, k2, k2 from cn; rep from * to last st, k1. **Row 6** Knit. **Row 8** K1, *sl 2 to cn and hold to *front*, k2, k2 from cn; rep from * to last st, k1.
Rep rows 1-8 for cable pat.

BACK
With larger needles, cast on 56 (62, 68, 74, 80, 86) sts. Work in cable pat for 16"/40.5cm, end with a WS row.

Armhole shaping
Bind off 4 sts at beg of next 2 rows, 1 st at beg of next 4 rows—44 (50, 56, 62, 68, 74) sts. Cont even in pat until armhole measures 9 (10, 10, 10, 11, 11)"/23 (25.5, 25.5, 25.5, 28, 28)cm, end with a WS row.

Shoulder shaping
Bind off 6 (7, 8, 9, 10, 11) sts at beg of next 4 rows. Bind off rem 20 (22, 24, 26, 28, 30) sts.

LEFT FRONT
With larger needles, cast on 32 (32, 38, 38, 44, 44) sts. Work in cable pat for 16"/40.5cm, end with a WS row.

Armhole shaping
Bind off at armhole edge 4 sts once, 1 st twice, AT SAME TIME, dec 1 st at neck edge every other row 14 (12, 16, 14, 18, 16) times—12 (14, 16, 18, 20, 22) sts. Cont even in pat until same

length as back to shoulder. Shape shoulder as for back.

RIGHT FRONT
Work as for left front, reversing all shapings.

SLEEVES
With larger needles, cast on 26 (32, 32, 32, 38, 38) sts. Work in cable pat, AT SAME TIME, inc 1 st each side every 4th row 14 times—54 (60, 60, 60, 66, 66) sts. Work even in pat until piece measures 18"/45.5 from beg.

Cap shaping
Bind off 4 sts at beg of next 2 rows, 2 sts at beg of next 6 rows—34 (40, 40, 40, 46, 46) sts. Bind off.

FINISHING
Block pieces to measurements. Sew shoulder seams. Set in and sew sleeves. Sew side and sleeve seams. With RS facing and crochet hook, work 1 row reverse sc (from left to right) evenly around all edges. Sew on hook and eyes, the first one at the beg of neck shaping, the second one 6"/15cm below. Attach collar.

(Schematics on page 127)

White Heat

for beginner knitters

Celebrate the holidays in white-hot style with this Norah Gaughan design that's big on texture, long on ease. A generous fit knit in luscious white Lopi, this sweater's drop sleeves focus on comfort, while a split neck and textural stitching gives it a fresh, modern feel. "White Heat" first appeared in the Winter '98/'99 issue of *Family Circle Easy Knitting*.

MATERIALS
- *Bulky Lopi* by Reynolds/JCA, 1³⁄₄oz/50g skeins, each approx 67yd/60m (wool)
  9 (10, 12, 13) skeins in #601 cream
- One pair each sizes 11 and 13 (8 and 9mm) needles OR SIZE TO OBTAIN GAUGE
- Size 11 (8mm) circular needle, 24"/60cm long

SIZES
Sized for Medium (Large, X-Large, XX-Large). Shown in size Medium.

FINISHED MEASUREMENTS
- Bust 42¹⁄₂ (49, 55, 62)"/107.5 (124.5, 139.5, 157.5)cm
- Length 27¹⁄₄ (27³⁄₄, 28³⁄₄, 29¹⁄₄)"/69 (70.5, 73, 74.5)cm
- Upper arm 16¹⁄₂ (17¹⁄₄, 18, 19)"/42 (44, 45.5, 48)cm

GAUGE
10 sts and 13 rows to 4"/10cm over pat st using larger needles.
TAKE TIME TO CHECK YOUR GAUGE.

PATTERN STITCH
(multiple of 8 sts plus 5)
Rows 1, 3 and 5 (RS) *P2, k1, p2, k3; rep from *, end p2, k1, p2.
Rows 2, 4 and 6 K2, p1, k2, *p3, k2, p1, k2; rep from * to end.
Rows 7, 9 and 11 P1, *k3, p2, k1, p2; rep from *, end k3, p1.
Rows 8, 10 and 12 K1, p3, *k2, p1, k2, p3; rep from *, end k1.

Rep rows 1-12 for pat st.

BACK
With larger needles, cast on 53 (61, 69, 77) sts. Work in pat st until piece measures 17"/43cm from beg.

Armhole shaping
Bind off 2 sts at beg of next 2 rows, bind off 1 st at beg of next 4 (4, 6, 8) rows—45 (53, 59, 65) sts. Work even until armhole measures 8¹⁄₂ (9, 10, 10¹⁄₂)"/21.5 (23, 25.5, 26.5)cm.

Neck and shoulder shaping
Bind off 5 (5, 7, 8) sts at beg of next 2 rows, 4 (6, 6, 7) sts at beg of next 4 rows, AT SAME TIME, bind off center 11 (11, 13, 13) sts and working both sides at once, bind of 2 sts from each neck edge twice.

FRONT
Work as for back until armhole measures 4 (4¹⁄₂, 5¹⁄₂, 6)"/10 (11.5, 14, 15)cm.

Divide for neck opening
Next row (RS) Work 22 (26, 29, 32) sts, join 2nd skein of yarn and bind off center st, work to end. Work both sides at once with separate skeins for 2¹⁄₂"/6.5cm.

Neck shaping
Bind off from each neck edge every other row 3 sts 1 (1, 2, 2) times, 2 sts 2 (2, 1, 1) time, 1 st twice, AT SAME TIME, when same length as back, shape shoulders as for back.

SLEEVES
With smaller needles, cast on 25 (25, 33, 33) sts.

Beg pat
Row 1 (RS) K2, (selvage sts) work pat st over next 21 (21, 29, 29) sts, k2 (selvage sts). Work in pat as established, inc 1 st each side (working incs into pat by M1 inside of k2 selvage sts) every 6th row 7 (5, 2, 6) times, then every 4th (4th, 8th, 8th) row 1 (4, 4, 1) times—41 (43, 45, 47) sts. Work even until piece measures 16 (16, 15, 15)"/40.5 (40.5, 38, 38)cm from beg.

Cap shaping
Bind off 3 sts at beg of next 2 rows, 2 sts at beg of next 6 (6, 2, 2) rows, 1 st at beg of next 0 (0, 4, 4) rows, 2 sts at beg of next 0 (0, 2, 2) rows, 3 sts at beg of next 2 rows. Bind off rem 17 (19, 21, 23) sts.

(Schematics on page 128)

Eye-Catching Eyelet

for intermediate knitters

Teva Durham turns the versatile V-neck into a knitted knockout using a zigzag eyelet stitch to mimic the neckline. Whether you pair it with pants or a skirt, wear it out day or night, this sleek design knows what it means to pair fashion and function. "Eye-Catching Eyelet" first appeared in the Fall '00 issue of *Family Circle Easy Knitting*.

MATERIALS

- *Sand* by Classic Elite Yarns, 1³/₄oz/50g balls each approx 77yd/70m (cotton) 17 (17, 19, 20, 22) balls in #6943 purple
- One pair each sizes 7 and 9 (4.5 and 5.5mm) needles OR SIZE TO OBTAIN GAUGE
- Size 7 (4.5mm) circular needle, 16"/40cm long
- Stitch markers

SIZES

Sized for Large (X-Large, 1X, 2X, 3X). Shown in size Large.

FINISHED MEASUREMENTS

- Bust 48 (52, 56, 60, 64)"/122 (132, 142, 152, 162.5)cm
- Length 26¹/₂ (27, 27¹/₂, 28, 28¹/₂)"/67 (68.5, 69.5, 71, 72)cm
- Upper arm 19 (20, 21, 22, 23)"/48 (51, 53, 56, 58)cm

GAUGE

16 sts and 23 rows to 4"/10cm over St st using larger needles.
TAKE TIME TO CHECK YOUR GAUGE.

Note

Be sure that there are the same number of yo's as decs on each row to keep stitch count the same. If not, then work these sts in St st instead of yo or dec.

STITCH GLOSSARY

Dec 2

Insert RH needle into next 2 sts as if to k2tog, but sl to RH needle without knitting, k the next st on LH needle, then with LH needle, pass both sts tog over st just knit.

SSSK

Sl next 3 sts knitwise, one at a time, to RH needle. Insert tip of LH needle into fronts of these sts from left to right. K them tog—2 sts dec.

BACK

With smaller needles, cast on 98 (106, 114, 122, 130) sts. Work in k2, p2 rib for 2¹/₂"/6.5cm, dec 1 st at end of last row—97 (105, 113, 121, 129) sts. Change to larger needles and work in St st for 2 rows.

Beg chart pat

Row 1 (RS) Beg with st 16 (12, 17, 13, 18) work to st 19, work sts 2 to 19 (18-st rep) 5 (5, 6, 6, 7) times, work sts 2 to 4 (8, 3, 7, 2). Cont in pat as established through chart row 16. *Work in St st for 12 rows. Work 16 rows of chart pat as before. Rep from * once more, then cont in St st until piece measures 26¹/₂ (27, 27¹/₂, 28, 28¹/₂)"/67 (68.5, 69.5, 71, 72)cm from beg. Bind off all sts.

FRONT

Work as for back until piece measures 21 (21¹/₂, 22, 22, 22¹/₂)"/53 (54.5, 55.5, 55.5, 56.5)cm from beg, end with a WS row.

Neck shaping

Next row (RS) Work 48 (52, 56, 60, 64) sts, join 2nd ball of yarn and bind off center st, work to end. Working both sides at once, work 1 row even. **Dec row 1 (RS)** Work to last 4 sts of first side, SSSK, k1; on 2nd side k1, k3tog, work to end. Rep dec row 1 every RS row 2 (3, 3, 3, 3)

times more. **Dec row 2 (RS)** Work to last 3 sts of first side, SSK, k1; on 2nd side k1, k2tog, work to end. Rep dec row 2 every RS row 10 (9, 9, 10, 10) times. Work even until same length as back. Bind off rem 31 (34, 38, 41, 45) sts each side for shoulders.

SLEEVES

With smaller needles, cast on 38 (38, 38, 42, 42) sts. Work in k2, p2 rib for 2¹/₂"/6.5cm, inc 1 (3, 3, 1, 1) st at end of last row—39 (41, 41, 43, 43) sts. Change to larger needles and work in St st for 2 rows.

Beg chart pat

Row 1 (RS) Beg with st 9 (8, 8, 7, 7) work to st 19, work sts 2 to 19 (18-st rep) once, work sts 2 to 11 (12, 12, 13, 13). Cont in pat as established through chart row 16. *Work in St st for 12 rows. Work 16 rows of lace chart as before. Rep from * once more, then cont in St st to end of piece, AT THE SAME TIME, inc 1 st each side (working inc sts into pat) every other row 0 (1, 5, 7, 11) times, then every 4th row 19 (19, 17, 16, 14) times—77 (81, 85, 89, 93) sts. Work even until piece measures 17"/43cm from beg. Bind off.

FINISHING

Block pieces to measurements. Sew shoulder seams.

(Continued on page 129)

Enchanted Evening

for intermediate crocheters

Anyone who says that crochet isn't elegant hasn't seen this romantic shawl draped over evening attire. Created simply by joining medallions, this offering from Norah Gaughan is a glamorous balance of winter warmth and skin-baring sensuality. "Enchanted Evening" first appeared in the Holiday '02 issue of *Family Circle Easy Knitting*.

MATERIALS
- *Fiora* by Adrienne Vittadini Yarns/JCA, .88oz/25g balls, each approx 52yd/48m (mohair/nylon/wool/polyester)
  9 balls in #31 plum
- Size J/10 (6mm) crochet hook OR SIZE TO OBTAIN GAUGE

SIZES
One size.

FINISHED MEASUREMENTS
- 18" x 39"/45.5 x 99cm

GAUGE
One medallion to 9"/23cm using size J/10 (6mm) crochet hook.
TAKE TIME TO CHECK YOUR GAUGE.

MEDALLION A
Ch 8. Join ch with a sl st forming a ring. **Rnd 1** Ch 3 (counts as 1 dc), work 23 dc in ring. Join rnd with a sl st in 3rd ch of ch-3. **Rnd 2** Ch 5 (counts as 1 dc and ch 2), sk first st, *dc in next st, ch 2, sk next st; rep from * around 11 times. Join rnd with a sl st in 3rd ch of ch-5—12 ch-2 sps. **Rnd 3** Ch 4 (counts as 1 tr), work 3 tr in first ch-2 sp, *work 4 tr in next ch-2 sp; rep from * around 11 times. Join rnd with a sl st in 4th ch of ch-4. **Rnd 4** Ch 3 (counts as 1 dc), [yo, draw up a lp in next st, yo and draw through 2 lps on hook] 3 times, yo and draw through all 4 lps on hook, ch 6, *dc in next st, [yo, draw up a lp in next st, yo and draw through 2 lps on hook] 3 times, yo and draw through all 4 lps on hook, ch 6; rep from * around 11 times. Join rnd with a sl st in 3rd ch of ch-3—12 ch-6 lps. **Rnd 5** Ch 1 (counts as 1 sc), work 3 sc in first ch-6 lp, ch 3, sl sl in last sc made (picot made), work 4 sc in same ch-6 lp, *work 4 sc in next ch-6 lp, ch 3, sl sl in last sc made, work 4 sc in same ch-6 lp; rep from * around 11 times. Join rnd with a sl st in first ch of ch-1. Fasten off.

MEDALLION B
(make 14)
Work as for medallion A to rnd 5. **Rnd 5** (join-ing) Ch 1 (counts as 1 sc), work 3 sc in first ch-6 lp, ch 3, sl sl in last sc made (picot made), work 4 sc in same ch-6 lp, * work 4 sc in next ch-6 lp, ch 3, sl sl in last sc made, work 4 sc in same ch-6 lp; rep from * around 9 times, end [work 4 sc in next ch-6 lp, ch 1, sc in picot of medallion A (joining st), ch 1, work 4 sc in same ch-6 lp] twice. Join rnd with a sl st in first ch of ch-1. Fasten off.

Referring to medallion placement diagram, join next medallion B (on rnd 5) to medallion A and to first medallion B, working picot sts and joining sts wherever needed. Cont to join 12 rem medallions together following diagram.

FINISHING
Lightly block piece to measurements.

(Schematics on page 129)

Urban Outfitter

for intermediate knitters

Big blocks of color bring Carla Scott's modest turtleneck to new levels of style in this high graphic design. Worked in gorgeous alpaca, this simple stockinette-stitch sweater with ribbed detail is both a unique piece and a fashion essential. "Urban Outfitter" first appeared in the Fall '02 issue of *Family Circle Easy Knitting*.

MATERIALS

- *Indiecita Baby Alpaca* by Plymouth Yarn, 1³/₄oz/50g balls, each approx 125yd/112m (alpaca)
  - 6 (6, 7, 7, 8) balls in #2020 burgundy (A)
  - 3 (3, 4, 4, 5) balls in #2050 red (B)
  - 2 (3, 3, 3, 4) balls #2010 rose (C)
- One pair each sizes 4 and 6 (3.5 and 4mm) needles OR SIZE TO OBTAIN GAUGE
- Size 4 (3.5mm) circular needle, 16"/40cm long

SIZES

Sized for Small (Medium, Large, X-Large, XX-Large). Shown in size Small.

FINISHED MEASUREMENTS

- Bust 36 (40, 44, 48, 52)"/91.5 (101.5, 111.5, 122, 132)cm
- Length 22 (22¹/₂, 23, 24, 24¹/₂)"/55.5 (57, 58, 60.5, 62)cm
- Upper arm 13 (14, 15¹/₂, 16¹/₂, 18)"/33 (35.5, 39.5, 42, 45.5)cm

GAUGE

24 sts and 30 rows to 4"/10cm over St st using larger needles.
TAKE TIME TO CHECK YOUR GAUGE.

Note

When changing colors, twist yarns on WS to prevent holes in work.

STITCH GLOSSARY

Single dec row

K2, k2tog, work to last 4 sts, SKP, k2.

Double dec row

K2, k3tog, work to last 5 sts, SK2P, k2.

BACK

With smaller needles and B, cast on 34 (37, 40, 44, 49) sts, with A, cast on 76 (85, 94, 102, 109) sts—110 (122, 134, 146, 158) sts. Work in k2, p2 rib, matching colors, for 2"/5cm, dec 2 sts in A section on last row. There are 34 (37, 40, 44, 49) B sts and 74 (83, 92, 100, 107) A sts for a total of 108 (120, 132, 144, 156) sts. Change to larger needles and work in St st and colors as established until piece measures 12¹/₂"/31.5cm from beg, end with a WS row.

Raglan armhole shaping

Bind off 5 sts at beg of next 2 rows. [Work double dec row, p 1 row] 0 (4, 8, 10, 14) times. [Work single dec row, p 1 row] 32 (29, 27, 28, 26) times. Bind off rem 34 (36, 36, 38, 38) sts for back neck.

FRONT

With smaller needles and A, cast on 76 (85, 94, 102, 109) sts, with B, cast on 34 (37, 40, 44, 49) sts—110 (122, 134, 146, 158) sts. Cont as for back until there are 44 (46, 46, 48, 48) sts.

Neck shaping

Next row (RS) Cont armhole shaping, bind off center 22 (24, 24, 26, 26) sts and working both sides at once, bind off from each neck edge 2 sts 3 times.

RIGHT SLEEVE

With smaller needles and A, cast on 46 (48, 48, 52, 52) sts. Work in k2, p2 rib for 3"/7.5cm, inc 5 sts evenly across last WS row—51 (53, 53, 57, 57) sts. Change to larger needles and work in St st, inc 1 st each side every 6th (6th, 4th, 4th, 4th) row 6 (14, 10, 11, 23) times, every 8th (8th, 6th, 6th, 6th) row 8 (2, 10, 10, 2) times—79 (85, 93, 99, 107) sts. Work even until piece measures 17 (17, 17, 17¹/₂, 17¹/₂)"/43 (43, 43, 44.5, 44.5)cm from beg. Place a marker each end of work. Work even for 1"/2.5cm more, end with a WS row.

Raglan cap shaping

[Work double dec row. P 1 row] 0 (2, 4, 4, 6) times. [Work single dec row. P 1 row] 33 (32, 32, 35, 35) times. Bind off rem 13 sts.

LEFT SLEEVE

Work same as right sleeve using C.

FINISHING

Block pieces to measurements. Sew raglan sleeve caps to raglan armholes, sewing 1"/2.5cm before sleeve cap to bound-off armhole sts on front and back. Sew side and sleeve seams.

Turtleneck

With RS facing, circular needle and B, pick up and k 100 (104, 104, 108, 108) sts evenly around neck edge. Join and work in k2, p2 rib for 6"/15.5cm. Bind off in rib.

(Schematics on page 130)

Faux Fabulous

Stitching up a stylish buttonless cardigan is a snap when you work with two strands of yarn held together. This subtly shaped design, knit in stockinette, is highlighted by whimsical faux fur trim along the edges. "Faux Fabulous" first appeared in the Holiday '03 issue of *Family Circle Easy Knitting*.

MATERIALS

- *Aspen* GGH/Muench Yarns, 1³⁄₄oz/50g balls, each approx 63yd/58m (wool/microfiber) 10 (10, 10, 11, 12) balls in #11 white (A)
- *Soft Kid* by GGH/Muench Yarns, .88oz/25g balls, each approx 151yd/138m (mohair/nylon/wool) 5 (5, 5, 6, 6) balls in #30 red (B)
- *Apart* by GGH/Muench Yarns, 1³⁄₄oz/50g balls, each approx 121yd/111m (nylon) 1 ball in #12 red (C)
- One pair size 11 (8mm) needles OR SIZE TO OBTAIN GAUGE

SIZES

Sized for Small (Medium, Large, X-Large, XX-Large). Shown in size Medium.

FINISHED MEASUREMENTS

- Bust (closed) 37 (40, 43, 48, 51)"/94 (101.5, 109, 122, 129.5)cm
- Waist (closed) 34 (37, 40, 43, 48)"/86 (94, 101.5, 109, 122)cm
- Length 22¹⁄₂ (23, 23³⁄₄, 24³⁄₄, 25¹⁄₂)"/57 (58.5, 60, 63, 65)cm
- Upper arm 17 (17¹⁄₂, 18¹⁄₂, 19¹⁄₄, 20)"/43 (44.5, 47, 49, 51)cm

GAUGE

10 sts and 15 rows to 4"/10cm over St st using 1 strand A and B held tog and size 11 (8mm) needles. TAKE TIME TO CHECK YOUR GAUGE.

Note

Work with 1 strand of A and B held tog.

BACK

With 1 strand A and B held tog, cast on 48 (52, 56, 62, 66) sts. **Row 1 (WS)** Knit. **Row 2 (RS)** With 2 strands C, knit. Change back to 1 strand A and B held tog and beg with a purl (WS) row, work in St st until piece measures 5"/13cm from beg. **Dec row (RS)** K5, k2tog, k to last 7 sts, SKP, k5. Rep dec row every 4th row twice more —42 (46, 50, 56, 60) sts. Work even until piece measures 11"/28cm from beg. **Inc row (RS)** K5, M1, k to last 5 sts, M1, k5. Rep inc row every 4th row once more—46 (50, 54, 60, 64) sts. Work even until piece measures 14 (14, 14¹⁄₂, 15, 15¹⁄₂)"/36 (36, 37, 38, 39)cm from beg.

Armhole shaping

Bind off 2 sts at beg of next 2 rows. **Dec row (RS)** K3, k2tog, k to last 5 sts, SKP, k3. Rep dec row every other row 3 times more—34 (38, 42, 48, 52) sts. Work even until armhole measures 7 (7¹⁄₂, 7³⁄₄, 8¹⁄₄, 8¹⁄₂)"/18 (19, 20, 21, 22)cm.

Beg neck trim

Next row (RS) K9 (11, 13, 15, 17), [p1, k1] 8 (8, 8, 9, 9) times, k to end. **Next row (WS)** P9 (11, 13, 15, 17), [k1, p1] 8 (8, 8, 9, 9) times, p to end.

Neck and shoulder shaping

Next row (RS) K6 (8, 10, 12, 14), [k1, p1] 3 times, join 2nd balls of yarn and bind off center 10 (10, 10, 12, 12) sts in seed st, then cont in seed st over the next 5 sts (1 st in seed st is left from binding off), k6 (8, 10, 12, 14). Cont to work each side with separate balls of yarn, bind off (in seed st) 3 sts from each neck edge once, AT SAME TIME, bind off 5 (5, 6, 7, 8) sts from each shoulder edge once and 4 (6, 7, 8, 9) sts once.

LEFT FRONT

With 1 strand A and B held tog, cast on 26 (28, 30, 33, 35) sts. **Row 1 (WS)** Knit. **Row 2 (RS)** With 2 strands C, k to last 3 sts, with 1 strand A and B held tog, p1, k1, p1. **Row 3 (WS)** With 1 strand A and B held tog, p1, k1, p1, 1 strand with C, p1, with 1 strand A and B held tog, p to end. Cont to work in this way, working the center front 4 sts in 1 St st with 2 strands C and 3 sts in seed st with 1 strand A and B, and the rem sts in 1 strand A and B in St st until piece measures 5"/13cm from beg. **Dec row (RS)** K5, k2tog, work as established to end. Rep dec row every 4th row twice more—23 (25, 27, 30, 32) sts. Work even until piece measures 11"/28cm from beg. **Inc row (RS)** K5, M1, work as established to end. Rep inc row every 4th row once more - 25 (27, 29, 32, 34) sts, AT SAME TIME, beg neck shaping when piece measures 12 (12, 12¹⁄₄, 12¹⁄₂, 13)"/30 (30, 31, 32, 33)cm from beg.

Neck shaping

Next row (RS) Work to last 6 sts, k2tog, work 4 sts of front band. Rep dec at neck edge every 4th row 9 (9, 9, 10, 10) times more, AT SAME TIME, when same length as back, work armhole shaping at beg of RS rows as for back. When armhole measures same as back, bind off 5 (5, 6, 7, 8) sts from shoulder edge once, 4 (6, 7, 8, 9) sts once.

(Continued on page 130)

Pullover Polish

for experienced knitters

Thanks to an interplay of color and texture, Irina Poludnenko's bell-sleeved pullover is anything but ordinary. A refreshing horizontal pattern and short-row shaping accentuate your figure, as well as reveal the hidden beauty of this purple-infused blue yarn. "Pullover Polish" first appeared in the Holiday '02 issue of *Family Circle Easy Knitting*.

MATERIALS

- *Mercury* by Colinette Yarns/Unique Kolours, 1³/₄oz/50g hanks, each approx 68yd/62m (viscose) 16 hanks in #93 lapis (MC)
- *Isis* by Colinette Yarns/Unique Kolours 3¹/₂oz/100g hanks, each approx 110yd/100m (viscose) 1 hank in #93 lapis (CC)
- One pair size 9 (5.5mm) needles OR SIZE TO OBTAIN GAUGE
- Size 9 (5.5mm) circular needle, 16"/40cm long.

SIZES
Sized for one size, Woman's Extra-Large.

FINISHED MEASUREMENTS
- Lower edge 56"/142cm
- Bust 44"/111.5cm
- Length 25"/63.5cm
- Upper arm 12"/30.5cm

GAUGE
16 sts and 21 rows to 4"/10cm over St st using size 9 (5.5mm) needles and Mercury.
TAKE TIME TO CHECK YOUR GAUGE.

Notes
1 Pullover pieces are worked from seam edge to seam edge with MC. The CC stripes are worked using the short row method (wrap and turn, w&t for flare shaping at lower edges).
2 Due to the unique stretchability of the yarn, only one size is written.

Short Row Wrapping
(wrap and turn - w&t)

Knit side
1 Wyib, sl next st purlwise.
2 Move yarn between the needles to the front.
3 Sl the same st back to LH needle. Turn work, bring yarn to the p side between needles. One st is wrapped. When short rows are completed, work to just before wrapped st, insert RH needle under the wrap and knitwise into the wrapped st, k them tog.

Purl side
1 Wyif, sl next st purlwise.
2 Move yarn between the needles to the back of work.
3 Sl same st back to LH needle. Turn work, bring yarn back to the p side between the needles. One st is wrapped. When short rows are completed, work to just before wrapped st, insert RH needle from behind into the back lp of the wrap and place on LH needle; P wrap tog with st on needle.

BACK
Beg at left side seam with MC, cast on 58 sts. Beg with a k row, work in St st for 8 rows. *Next row (RS) With MC, k to last st, inc 1 st in last st (for armhole shaping). With MC, purl 1 row.* Next (short) row (RS) With CC, k32, w&t. With CC, p to end. Rep between *'s 4 times more—63 sts. Next (short) row (RS) With CC, k 58, w&t. With CC, p to end. Next row (RS) With MC, knit 63 then cast on 29 sts (for straight armhole edge)—92 sts. With MC, work 7 rows in St st. Next (short) row (RS) With CC, k20, w&t. With CC, p to end. Next row (RS) With MC, k to last st, M1, k1—93sts. With MC, work 7 rows in St st. Next (short) row (RS) With CC, k 45, w&t. With CC, p to end. Next row (RS) With MC, k to last st, M1, k1—94 sts. With MC, work 7 rows in St st. Next (short) row (RS) With CC, k35, w&t. With CC, p to end.

Beg back neck
With MC, work 8 rows iin St st. Next (short) row (RS) With CC, k55, w&t. With CC, p to end. With MC, work 8 rows in St st. Next (short) row (RS) With CC, k25, w&t. With CC, p to end. With MC, work 8 rows in St st. Next (short) row (RS) With CC, k 65, w&t. With CC, p to end. With MC, work 8 rows in St st. Next (short) row (RS) With CC, K47, w&t. With CC, p to end. With +MC, work 6 rows in St st. Next row (RS) K to last 3 sts., k2tog, k1. Work 3 rows in St st. Next (short) row (RS) With CC, k55, w&t. With CC, p to end. With MC, k1 row. Next row (WS) With MC, bind off 29 sts, (for straight armhole edge), p to end—63 sts.**Next row K to llast 3 sts, k2tog, k1, p1 row**. Rep between **'s twice more—60 sts. Next (short) row (RS) With CC, k30, w&t, with CC, p to end. Rep between **'s twice more—58 sts. With MC, work in St st for 4 rows. Next (short) row (RS) With CC, k40, w&t. With CC, p to end. With MC, work in St st for 4 rows. Bind off 58 sts.

FRONT
Work as for back, only replace the back neck shaping(between +'s) as foll:

(Continued on page 131)

Fringed Benefits

for intermediate knitters

Melissa Leapman's sassy fringed design is fashionable and fun—the perfect match for a pair of lean jeans and daring boots. The horizontal garter ridges on the sleeves and turtleneck are playfully at odds with the vertically worked body, which is simultaneously smart and slimming. Warmth, style, originality—what more could you ask for in a sweater? "Fringed Benefits" first appeared in the Fall '02 issue of *Family Circle Easy Knitting*.

MATERIALS

- *14-Ply* by Wool Pak Yarns NZ/Baabajoes Wool Co., 8oz/250g hanks, each approx 310yd/286m (wool)
  4 (5, 5) hanks in #17 blue
- Size 9 (5.5mm) circular needle, 40"/100cm long OR SIZE TO OBTAIN GAUGE
- One each sizes 9 and 10 (5.5 and 6mm) circular needle, 16"/40cm long
- Stitch holders

SIZES

Sized for Small/Medium (Large, X/XX-Large). Shown in size Large.

FINISHED MEASUREMENTS

- Bust 43 (45, 48)"/109 (114, 122)cm
- Length 24 (24½, 25½)"/61 (62, 65)cm
- Upper arm 17½ (18½, 19½)"/44.5 (47, 49.5)cm

GAUGE

16 sts and 24 rows to 4"/10cm over ridge pat st using size 9 (5.5mm) needles.
TAKE TIME TO CHECK YOUR GAUGE.

RIDGE PATTERN STITCH

Rows 1-5 Knit.
Row 6 Purl.
Row 7 Knit
Row 8 Purl.
Rep rows 1-8 for ridge pat st.

Notes

1 Sweater is made all in one piece beg and end at sleeve cuff edges.
2 Lower edge fringe will be made after piece is knit by unraveling 6 sts at lower edges.

BODY

Beg at right sleeve cuff edge, with size 9 (5.5mm) circular needle, cast on 36 (38, 40) sts. Work in ridge pat st, inc 1 st each side every 4th row 6 (8, 10) times, every 6th row 11 (10, 9) times—70 (74, 78) sts. Work even until piece measures 16½ (16½, 17½)"/42 (42, 44.5)cm from beg, ending with row 2 of 13th (13th, 14th) ridge pat rep. Place yarn markers at beg and end of last row for side seam.

BACK AND FRONT

Cast on 61 (61, 63) sts at beg of next 2 rows—192 (196, 204) sts. Beg with row 5 of pat st, cont in ridge pat st for 6¾ (7½, 8)"/17 (19, 20.5)cm from side seam markers, end with pat row 2 (6, 2).

Divide for neck

Next row (RS) Work 92 (94, 98) sts and leave on a holder for front, bind off 4 sts and work to end—96 (98, 102) sts for back. Cont to work on these sts until there are 48 rows in back neck. Leave these sts on a holder. Return to sts for front and dec 1 st at neck edge on next row then every row once, every other row twice, every 4th row once—87 (89, 93) sts. Work even for 28 rows. Inc 1 st at neck edge on next row then every 4th row once, every other row twice, every row once—92 (94, 98) sts.

JOIN FRONT AND BACK

Next row (RS) Work sts of back, cast on 4 sts at neck edge, work sts of front—192 (196, 204) sts. Cont to work as for first side, ending with row 2 of pat st. Bind off 61 (61, 63) sts at beg of next 2 rows. Cont on 70 (74, 78) sts for sleeve, dec 1 st on corresponding row to match left sleeve inc—36 (38, 40) sts. K 4 rows to complete sleeve and bind off.

FINISHING

Block pieces to measurements.

Collar

With RS facing and smaller 16"/40cm circular needle, pick up and k 74 sts evenly around neck edge. Join and work in rnds as foll: [K 1 rnd, p 1 rnd] twice, k 4 rnds. Rep these 8 rnds once for ridge pat st. **Next rnd** Knit, inc 8 sts evenly around—82 sts. Work even for 11/2"/4cm more. Change to larger 16"/40cm circular needle and work in pat st until collar measures 8"/20.5cm from beg. Bind off loosely. Cut two 7"/18cm lengths of yarn for each fringe and attach 1 fringe every ½"/1.5cm around collar. Sew side and sleeve seams.

Lower edge fringe

Unravel 6 sts at lower edges of front and back and cut loops of each st at center. Then tie 2 ends tog using overhand knot to secure. Trim fringe evenly.

(Schematics on page 131)

Autumn Harvest

for intermediate knitters

There is nothing that captures soft sensuality like mohair, and this artful design is no exception. Worked in an autumnal orange with occasional stripes of novelty yarn that play up mohair's fuzzy characteristics, this is a chic way to celebrate the timeless traditions of the fall season. "Autumn Harvest" first appeared in the Fall '03 issue of *Family Circle Easy Knitting*.

MATERIALS

- *Mohair Kiss* by DiVe/LBUSA, 1³/₄oz/50g balls, each approx 98yd/90m (mohair/wool/polyamide) 11 (12, 14, 16, 18) balls in #19233 orange (A)
- *Grand Duchess* by Tawny/LBUSA, 1³/₄ oz/50g balls, each approx 50yd/46m (polyester) 2 balls in #2057 multi (B)
- One pair size 7 (4.5mm) needles OR SIZE TO OBTAIN GAUGE

SIZES

Sized for Small (Medium, Large, X-Large, XX-Large). Shown in size Medium.

FINISHED MEASUREMENTS

- Lower edge 40 (43, 45, 49, 51¹/₂)"/101.5 (109, 114, 124.5, 131)cm
- Bust 38 (41, 43, 47, 50)"/96.5 (104, 109, 119, 127)cm
- Length 23³/₄ (24¹/₂, 25, 26, 26¹/₂)"/60 (62, 63.5, 66, 67.5)cm
- Upper arm 14³/₄ (15³/₄, 16¹/₂, 17, 17¹/₂)"/37.5 (40, 42, 43, 44.5)cm

GAUGE

18 sts and 26 rows to 4"/10cm over St st using size 7 (4.5mm) needles.
TAKE TIME TO CHECK YOUR GAUGE.

BACK

Note Read before beg to knit.

With size 7 (4.5mm) needles and B, cast on 90 (96, 102, 110, 116) sts. K 2 rows. Change to A and work in stripes as foll: *Work 12 rows in St st with A, k 2 rows with B; rep from * twice more then, **work 18 rows in St st with A, k 2 rows with B; rep from ** twice more, then cont with A only in St st to end of piece, AT SAME TIME, when piece measures 2¹/₂"/6.5cm from beg, dec 1 st each side of row. Rep dec every 12th row 4 times more—80 (86, 92, 100, 106) sts. Work even until piece measures 12"/30cm from beg. Inc 1 st each side of next row and rep inc every 10th row once, every 8th row once— 86 (92, 98, 106, 112) sts. Work even until piece measures 15¹/₂ (15³/₄, 16, 16¹/₂, 16¹/₂)"/39 (40, 41, 42, 42) cm from beg.

Armhole shaping

Bind off 5 sts at beg of next 4 rows—66 (72, 78, 86, 92) sts. Work even until armhole measures 7³/₄ (8¹/₄, 8¹/₂, 9, 9¹/₂)"/20 (21, 22, 23, 24) cm.

Shoulder shaping

Bind off 7 (8, 9, 11, 12) sts at beg of next 2 rows, 7 (8, 10, 11, 13) sts at beg of next 2 rows—38 (40, 40, 42, 42) sts. Work even on these sts for 2³/₄"/7cm for collar. Bind off.

FRONT

Work as for back.

SLEEVES

With needles and B, cast on 62 (64, 66, 68, 70) sts. K 2 rows. Change to A and cont in St st for 16 rows more. **Dec row (RS)** K13 (14, 15, 16, 17), *pm, k2tog, k15; rep from * once more, pm, k2tog, k13 (14, 15, 16, 17). Rep dec row every 18th row twice more, working 3 decs after markers each dec row—53 (55, 57, 59, 61) sts. Work even until piece measures 10"/25cm from beg. Inc 1 st each side of next row and rep inc alternately every 4th and 6th row until there are—67 (71, 75, 77, 79) sts. Work even until piece measures 17¹/₂ (17³/₄, 18, 18¹/₂, 18¹/₂)"/44 (45, 46, 47, 47) cm from beg.

Cap shaping

Next row Dec 1 st at beg and end of row. Work 1 row even. Rep last 2 rows 6 times more. Bind off rem 53 (57, 61, 63, 65) sts.

FINISHING

Block pieces to measurements. Sew shoulder seams. Set in sleeves. Sew side and sleeve seams.

(Schematics on page 132)

Blue Cross

Cozy, classic, and cabled, this Linda Cyr design is a solid addition to any wardrobe. Simple reverse stockinette stitch lets you focus your energy on the crossed and straight cables running down the front and sleeves; a chunky turtleneck sports spiffy ribbing. "Blue Cross" first appeared in the Fall '02 issue of *Family Circle Easy Knitting*.

MATERIALS

- *Kool Wool* by Lion Brand Yarn Co., 1³/₄oz/50g balls, each approx 60yd/54m (wool/acrylic) 18 (20, 22) balls in #109 blue
- One pair size 10 (6mm) needles OR SIZE TO OBTAIN GAUGE
- Cable needles (cn)
- Stitch holders

SIZES

Sized for Large (1X, 2X). Shown in size Large.

FINISHED MEASUREMENTS

- Bust 46 (50, 54)"/117 (127, 137)cm
- Length 26"/66cm
- Upper arm 16 (17, 18)"/40 (43, 45.5)cm

GAUGE

13 sts and 19 rows to 4"/10cm over St st using size 10 (6mm) needles.
TAKE TIME TO CHECK YOUR GAUGE.

STITCH GLOSSARY AND STITCHES

K2, P2 rib

Row 1 (RS) *K2, p2; rep from * to end.
Row 2 K the knit and p the purl sts.
Rep row 2 for k2, p2 rib.

Front cable (FC)

Row 1 K4.
Rows 2 and 4 P4.
Row 3 Sl 2 sts to cn and hold to *front*, k2, k2 from cn.
Rep rows 1-4 for FC.

Back cable (BC)

Row 1 K4.
Rows 2 and 4 P4.
Row 3 Sl 2 sts to cn and hold to *back*, k2, k2 from cn.
Rep rows 1-4 for BC.

Front traveling cable (FTC)

Row 1 Work to FC, sl 4 sts to cn and hold to *front*, p2, k4 from cn.
Rows 2 and 4 P4.
Row 3 Sl 2 sts to cn and hold to *front*, k2, k2 from cn.
Rep rows 1-4 for FTC.

Back traveling cable (BTC)

Row 1 Work to 2 sts before BC, sl 2 sts to cn and hold to *back*, k4, p2 from cn.
Rows 2 and 4 Purl.
Row 3 Sl 2 sts to cn and hold to *back*, k2, k2 from cn.
Rep rows 1-4 for BTC.

BACK

Cast on 82 (90, 98) sts.
Row 1 (RS) Work k2, p2 rib over 12 (16, 20) sts, FC, p2, work k2, p2 rib over 48 sts, BC, p2, work k2, p2 rib over 8 (12, 16) sts, end k2. Cont in pat as established for 2¹/₂"/6.5cm, end with a WS row. **Next row (RS)** P12 (16, 20), work FC, ssk, k46, k2tog, work BC, p12 (16, 20)—80 (88, 96) sts. **Next row** K12 (16, 20), work BC, p48, work FC, k12 (16, 20). **Next row** P12 (16, 20), work FC, k48, work BC, p12 (16, 20). **Next row** K12 (16, 20), work BC, p48, work FC, k12 (16, 20).

Beg traveling cables

Next row (RS) P12 (16, 20), FTC, k44, BTC, p12

(16, 20). **Next row (WS)** K the knit and p the purl sts. Cont to work FTC and BTC as established, moving 2 purl sts to right of FTC and 2 purl sts to left of BTC until the FC and BC meet with 8 cable sts at center, end with a WS row 2 of pat. **Next row (RS)** P36 (40, 44), work row 3 of FC, row 3 of BC, p36 (40, 44).
Next row K36 (40, 44), p8, k36 (40, 44). **Next row** P36 (40, 44), k8, p36 (40, 44). **Next row** K36 (40, 44), p8, k36 (40, 44). Rep last 2 rows once. **Next row** K36 (40, 44), work row 3 of BC, row 3 of FC, k36 (40, 44). **Next row** K36 (40, 44), p8, k36 (40, 44). **Next row** P34 (38, 42), BTC only k2 from cn instead of p2, FTC only k2 instead of p2, p34 (38, 42). Cont to work in this way displacing cables and working central sts as knit until piece measures 16 (15¹/₂, 15)"/40 (39.5, 38)cm from beg.

Armhole shaping

Bind off 4 (5, 6) sts at beg of next 2 rows. Dec 1 st each side every other row 3 (3, 4) times, every 4th row 1 (2, 2) times—64 (68, 72) sts. Work even until armhole measures 8³/₄ (9¹/₄, 9³/₄)"/22 (23.5, 25)cm.

Shoulder shaping

Bind off 6 (7, 7) sts at beg of next 4 rows, 8 (7, 8) sts at beg of next 2 rows. Bind off rem 24 (26, 28) sts for back neck.

(Continued on page 132)

Cable Vision

for intermediate knitters

A zippered crewneck cardigan, designed by Diane Zangl, is a wardrobe basic. But what happens when you introduce a little bit of interlacing cables and a whole lot of bold color? You get a sporty-yet-sophisticated number that can go urban or suburban in an instant. "Cable Vision" first appeared in the Winter '97/'98 issue of *Family Circle Easy Knitting*.

MATERIALS
- *Wool Pak 10 Ply* by Baabajoes Wool Co./Wool Pak Yarns NZ, 8oz/250g balls, each approx 430yd/397m (wool)
  4 (4, 4, 4) balls in #36 paprika
- One pair each sizes 4 and 6 (3.5 and 4mm) needles OR SIZE TO OBTAIN GAUGE
- Size 4 (3.5mm) circular needle, 16"/40cm long
- Stitch markers and stitch holders
- 18 (20, 20, 20)"/46 (51, 51, 51)cm separating zipper
- Cable needle (cn)

SIZES
Sized for Small (Medium, Large, X-Large). Shown in size Medium.

FINISHED MEASUREMENTS
- Bust (closed) 38 (41½, 44½, 48)"/96.5 (105.5, 113, 122)cm
- Length 21 (22, 23, 23½)"/53.5 (56, 58.5, 59.5)cm
- Upper arm 16 (17, 18, 19)"/40.5 (43, 46, 48)cm

GAUGE
- 19 sts and 25 rows to 4"/10 cm over St st, using larger needles.
- 30 sts of Cable chart to 4½"/11.5cm wide, using larger needles.

TAKE TIME TO CHECK YOUR GAUGE.

STITCH GLOSSARY
2/1 Right Purl Cross (2/1 RPC) Sl 1 st to cn and hold to *back*, k2, p1 from cn.
2/1 Left Purl Cross (2/1 LPC) Sl 2 sts to cn and hold to *front*, p1, k2 from cn.
2/2 Right Cable (2/2 RC) Sl 2 sts to cn and hold to *back*, k2, k2 from cn.
2/2 Left Cable (2/2 LC) Sl 2 sts to cn and hold to *front*, k2, k2 from cn.
2/2 Right Purl Cross (2/2 RPC) Sl 2 sts to cn and hold to *back*, k2, p2 from cn.
2/2 Left Purl Cross (2/2 LPC) Sl 2 sts to cn and hold to *front*, p2, k2 from cn.

Twisted rib
(odd number of sts)
Row 1 (RS) K1 through back lp (tbl), *p1, k1 tbl; rep from * to end.
Row 2 P1 tbl, *k1, p1 tbl; rep from * to end.
Rep rows 1 and 2 for twisted rib.

BACK
With smaller needles, cast on 99 (103, 111, 119) sts. Work in twisted rib for 2"/5cm, inc 17 (19, 19, 21) sts evenly across last (WS) row—116 (122, 130, 140) sts. Change to larger needles.
Beg chart
Row 1 (RS) K13 (16, 20, 25), [work row 1 of Cable chart over 30 sts] 3 times, k13 (16, 20, 25). Cont in pat as established, working center 90 sts into cable pat and rem sts in St st, until piece measures 13 (13½, 14, 14)"/33 (34, 35.5, 35.5)cm from beg, end with a WS row.
Armhole shaping
Bind off 7 (8, 9, 10) sts at beg of next 2 rows. Dec 1 st each side on next row, then every other row 3 (3, 3, 4) times more—94 (98, 104, 110) sts. Work even until armhole measures 7 (7½, 8, 8½)"/18 (19, 20.5, 21.5)cm, end with a WS row.
Neck shaping
Next row (RS) Work 30 (31, 32, 33) sts, join 2nd ball of yarn and bind off center 34 (36, 40, 44) sts, work to end. Working both sides at once, dec 1 st at each neck edge every row 3 times. Bind off rem 27 (28, 29, 30) sts each side for shoulders.

LEFT FRONT
With smaller needles, cast on 49 (51, 55, 59) sts. Work twisted rib, slipping first st of every WS row, for 2"/5cm, end with a RS row. **Next row (WS)** Rib 9 (front band), then rib to end, inc 8 (10, 10, 10) sts evenly across—57 (61, 65, 69) sts. Change to larger needles.
Beg chart
Next row (RS) K13 (16, 20, 25), work row 1 of Cable chart over 30 sts, k5 (6, 6, 5), rib 9. Cont in pat as established until same length as back to underarm. Shape armhole at beg of RS rows as for back—46 (49, 52, 54) sts. Work even until armhole measures 5 (5½, 6, 6 ½)"/12.5 (14, 15, 16.5)cm, end with a RS row.

Neck shaping
Next row (WS) Work 14 (16, 18, 19) sts in pat and sl these sts to a holder, work to end. Cont in pat, dec 1 st at neck edge on next row, then every other row 4 times more. Work even until same length as back to shoulder. Bind off rem 27 (28, 29, 30) sts.

RIGHT FRONT
Work as for left front, reversing all shaping and placement of pats.

(Continued on page 133)

Sheer Delight

for intermediate knitters

Irina Poludnenko's design is proof that not all crewnecks are created equal. A combination of ladder and garter slip-stitch motifs results in a delicate play of stripes and squares that works any time of year. "Sheer Delight" first appeared in the Winter '01/'02 issue of *Family Circle Easy Knitting*.

MATERIALS

- *Passion* by Garnstudio/Aurora Yarns, 1³/₄oz/50g balls, each approx 108yd/100m (wool/viscose/polyamide)
  7 (8, 10) balls in #1 cream
- One pair size 7 (4.5mm) needles OR SIZE TO OBTAIN GAUGE
- Stitch holders
- Size 7 (4.5mm) circular needle, 16"/40cm long

SIZES

Sized for Medium/Large (X-Large, XX-Large) Shown in size Medium/Large.

FINISHED MEASUREMENTS

- Bust 40 (47, 55)"/101.5 (119, 139.5)cm
- Length 23 (24¹/₂, 26)"/58.5 (62, 66)cm
- Upper arm 13 (15, 17)"/33 (38, 43)cm

GAUGE

14 sts and 28 rows to 4"/10cm over pat st foll chart using size 7 (4.5mm) needles.
TAKE TIME TO CHECK YOUR GAUGE.

Note

Sts 1 and 20 of chart are selvage sts and not figured into the measurements.

BACK

Cast on 72 (85, 98) sts. Work in k1, p1 rib for 1"/2.5cm.

Beg pat st

Row 1 (WS) Foll chart from left to right, beg with st 20, work through st 1, then rep sts 14-2 for 4 (5, 6) times more. Cont to foll chart in this way, rep rows 1-12 until piece measures 14 (14¹/₂, 15)"/35.5 (37, 38)cm from beg.

Armhole shaping

Bind off 4 (4, 5) sts at beg of next 2 rows, 3 sts at beg of next 2 rows, 2 sts at beg of next 2 (2, 4) rows, dec 1 st each side every other row 1 (3, 3) times—52 (61, 68) sts. Work even until armhole measures 8 (9, 10)"/20.5 (23, 25.5)cm.

Neck and shoulder shaping

Bind off 5 (6, 7) sts at beg of next 4 rows, 4 (5, 6) sts at beg of next 2 rows. Sl rem 24 (27, 28) sts to a holder for back neck.

FRONT

Work as for back until armhole measures 6 (7, 8)"/15 (18, 20.5)cm.

Neck shaping

Next row (RS) Work 24 (27, 30) sts, join a 2nd ball of yarn and bind off center 4 (7, 8) sts, work to end. Working both sides at once, bind off 4 sts from each neck edge once, 3 sts once, 2 sts once and 1 st once—14 (17, 20) sts rem each side. When same length as back, shape shoulders as on back.

SLEEVES

Cast on 33 sts. Work in k1, p1 rib for 1"/2.5cm, end with a RS row.

Beg pat st

Row 1 (WS) Foll chart from left to right, beg with st 20, work through st 1, then rep sts 14-2 once. Cont to foll chart in this way, inc 1 st each side every 10th (8th, 6th) row 7 (10, 14) times—47 (53, 61) sts. Work even until piece measures 17 (17¹/₂, 18)"/43 (44.5, 45.5)cm from beg.

Cap shaping

Bind off 3 (3, 4) sts at beg of next 2 rows, 2 sts at beg of next 2 rows. Dec 1 st each side every other row 11 (14, 17) times. Bind off rem 15 sts.

FINISHING

Block pieces to measurements. Sew shoulder seams.

Neckband

With circular needle, pick up and k 66 (72, 74) sts evenly around neck edge. Join and work in k1, p1 rib for 1"/2.5cm. Bind off in rib. Set in sleeves. Sew side and sleeve seams.

(Schematics on page 133)

Soak Up the Sun

Cool down with these breezy styles for balmy weather.

In Bloom

Whether it's a walk on the beach or shopping on the boardwalk, Teva Durham's carefree tunic is a vacation necessity. Featuring eyelet zigzags and a kiss of pink embroidered flowers, this is the ideal design to beat the heat. "In Bloom" first appeared in the Spring/Summer '00 issue of *Family Circle Easy Knitting*.

MATERIALS

- *Sand* by Classic Elite Yarns, 1¾oz/50g balls, each approx 77yd/70m (cotton)
  15 (17, 19, 21) balls in #6492 lt blue (MC)
- *Embroidery Floss* by DMC, 6m skeins
  2 skeins each in #275 white (A), #150 dk blue (B), #139 med blue (C), #146 lt blue (D), #110 dk violet (E) and #108 lt violet (F)
- One pair each sizes 8 and 9 (5 and 5.5mm) needles OR SIZE TO OBTAIN GAUGE
- Size G/6 (4.5mm) crochet hook

SIZES

Sized for Small/Medium (Large, X-Large, XX-Large). Shown in size Small/Medium.

FINISHED MEASUREMENTS

- Bust 45 (50, 54, 59)"/114 (127, 137, 150)cm
- Length 27½ (28, 28½, 29)"/70 (71, 72.5, 73.5)cm
- Upper arm 21 (22, 23, 24)"/53 (56, 58.5, 61)cm

GAUGE

16 sts and 23 rows to 4"/10cm over St st using larger needles OR over pointelle pat foll chart using smaller needles.
TAKE TIME TO CHECK YOUR GAUGE.

STITCH GLOSSARY

Dec 2

Insert RH needle into next 2 sts as if to k2tog, but sl to RH needle without knitting, k the next st on LH needle, then with LH needle, pull both sts over st just knit.

BACK

With smaller needles and MC, cast on 91 (101, 109, 119) sts. P 1 row on WS.

Beg chart

Row 1 (RS) Work 0 (5, 0, 5) sts in St st, work st 1 of chart then work 18-st rep 5 (5, 6, 6) times, work 0 (5, 0, 5) sts in St st. Cont in pat as established through row 55 of chart. Change to larger needles and cont in St st until piece measures 17½"/44.5cm from beg.

Armhole shaping

Dec 1 st each side every row 3 times, then each side every other row 4 times—77 (87, 95, 105) sts. Work even until armhole measures 10 (10½, 11, 11½)"/25.5 (26.5, 28, 29)cm. Bind off.

FRONT

Work as for back until armhole measures 4½ (5, 5½, 6)"/11.5 (12.5, 14, 15)cm.

Neck shaping

Next row (RS) Work 37 (42, 46, 51) sts, join 2nd ball of yarn and bind off center 3 sts, work to end. Working both sides at once, dec 1 st each side of neck every row 9 times, then every other row 9 times—19 (24, 28, 33) sts each side for shoulders. When same length as back to shoulders, bind off.

SLEEVES

With larger needles and MC, cast on 46 (48, 48, 50) sts. Cont in St st, inc 1 st each side every 6th row 8 (6, 2, 0) times, every 4th row 11 (14, 20, 23) times—84 (88, 92, 96) sts. Work even until piece measures 17½"/44.5cm from beg.

Cap shaping

Work as for back armhole shaping—70 (74, 78, 82) sts. Bind off.

FINISHING

Block pieces to measurements. Sew shoulder seams. With crochet hook, work an edge of sc evenly around neck edge.

Embroidery

With C and foll upper zigzag of chart pat, work chain stitch embroidery at 1½"/4cm above the pointelle pat. Alternating A, E, and F, work 5-point lazy daisy sts at each point of zigzag. Work French knot centers in alternating colors. With C and D, work lazy daisy leaves along starting zigzag lines and fill in each leaf with A in straight st. Sew sleeves into armholes. Sew side and sleeve seams.

(Schematics on page 134)

The Floridian

Rediscover garter stitch with this fine warm-weather design from Irina Poludnenko. Capped sleeves form a charming open neckline, while the combination of bright yellow and pastel purple delivers a stylish taste of the tropics. "The Floridian" first appeared in the Spring/Summer '03 issue of *Family Circle Easy Knitting*.

MATERIALS

- *Star* by Classic Elite Yarns, 1³⁄₄oz/50g balls, each approx 127yd/115m (cotton/lycra)
  5 (6, 7, 8, 9) balls in #5108 purple (MC)
  1 (1, 1, 2, 2) balls in #5135 yellow (CC)
- One pair size 8 (5mm) needles OR SIZE TO OBTAIN GAUGE

SIZES

Sized for Small (Medium, Large, X-Large, XX-Large). Shown in size Small.

FINISHED MEASUREMENTS

- Bust 34 (37, 40, 44, 47)"/86 (94, 101.5, 111.5, 119)cm
- Length 19¹⁄₂ (20¹⁄₄, 20³⁄₄, 21¹⁄₂, 22)"/49.5 (51.5, 52.5, 54.5, 56)cm
- Upper arm 15 (17, 17¹⁄₂, 19¹⁄₂, 20¹⁄₄)"/38 (43, 44.5, 49.5, 51.5)cm

GAUGE

19 sts and 38 rows to 4"/10cm over garter st using size 8 (5mm) needles.
TAKE TIME TO CHECK YOUR GAUGE.

BACK

With MC, cast on 80 (88, 96, 104, 112) sts. Working in garter st (k every row), work even until piece measures 12"/30.5cm from beg.

Raglan armhole shaping

Dec row (RS) K2, k2tog, k to end. Rep dec row every row 37 (45, 49, 57, 61) times more. Bind off rem 42 (42, 46, 46, 50) sts for back neck.

FRONT

Work as for back.

SLEEVES

With CC, cast on 72 (80, 84, 92, 96) sts. K2 rows.

Raglan cap shaping

Dec row (RS) K2, k2tog, k to end.
Rep dec row every row 37 (45, 49, 57, 61) times more. Bind off rem 34 sts.

FINISHING

Sew raglan sleeves into raglan armholes. Sew side seams.

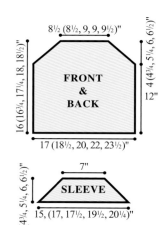

High Splits

for beginner knitters

This split shoulder scoop neck top from designer Norah Gaughan adds a snazzy twist to summer style. Worked in a stockinette stitch using a luscious purple nylon/cotton blend, this design shows off shoulders in a delightfully offbeat way. "High Splits" first appeared in the Spring/Summer '03 issue of *Family Circle Easy Knitting*.

MATERIALS

- *Cinema* by Artful Yarns/JCA, 1³⁄₄oz/50g balls, each approx 110yd/99m (nylon/cotton)
  6 (7, 7, 8 , 9) balls in #194 purple
- One pair size 8 (5mm) needles OR SIZE TO OBTAIN GAUGE
- Size G/6 (4.5mm) crochet hook

SIZES

Sized for Small (Medium, Large, X-Large, XX-Large). Shown in size Medium.

FINISHED MEASUREMENTS

- Bust 36 (38¹⁄₂, 40, 46¹⁄₂, 50¹⁄₂)"/91 (98, 101.5, 118, 128)cm
- Length 22 (22, 22¹⁄₂, 23, 23¹⁄₂)"/56 (56, 57, 58.5, 59.5)cm

GAUGE

20 sts and 24 rows to 4"/10cm over St st using size 8 (5mm) needles.
TAKE TIME TO CHECK YOUR GAUGE.

BACK

Cast on 90 (96, 100, 116, 126) sts. Work in St st for 15"/38cm.

Beg sleeves

Cast on 5 sts at beg of next 2 rows—100 (106, 110, 126, 136) sts. Work even for 2 (2, 6, 6, 6) rows. **Inc row (RS)** K3, M1, k to last 3 sts, M1, k3. Rep inc row every 6th row 6 times more— 114 (120, 124, 140, 150) sts. Work even until armhole measures 7 (7, 7¹⁄₂, 8, 8¹⁄₂)"/18 (18, 19, 20.5, 21.5)cm from cast-on edge, end with a WS row.

Neck and shoulder shaping

Bind off 32 (35, 37, 44, 48) sts at beg of next row for right shoulder. Bind off rem 82 (85, 87, 96, 102) sts for left shoulder and back neck.

FRONT

Work as for back until piece measures 20 (20, 20¹⁄₂, 21, 21¹⁄₂)"/51 (51, 52, 53.5, 54.5)cm from beg. Mark center 40 (40, 40, 42, 44) sts for neck.

Neck shaping

Next row (RS) Work to center marked neck sts, join 2nd ball of yarn and bind off center 40 (40, 40, 42, 44) sts, work to end. Work both sides at once for 1 row more. **Dec row (RS)** Work to last 5 sts of first side, ssk, k3; on 2nd side, k3, k2tog, k to end. Rep dec row every other row 4 times more—32 (35, 37, 44, 48) sts rem each side. When same length as back, bind off rem sts each side for shoulders.

FINISHING

Leaving the last 22 (25, 27, 30, 34) sts open for the flutter sleeve, sew tog 10 (10, 10, 14, 14) sts of front and back shoulders from the neck edge. Sew side seams and the 5-st bound-offs tog at underarms. With crochet hook, work an edge of reverse sc (working from left to right) around neck edge.

(Schematics on page 134)

This delightful summer top from Mari Lynn Patrick is proof that style can indeed be effortless. Worked in pastel pink chenille, this sleeveless number is simply two squares knitted and sewn together for a quick and easy summer sweater. "Think Pink" first appeared in the Spring/Summer '99 issue of *Family Circle Easy Knitting*.

MATERIALS

■ *Grace* by Patons® 1³/₄ oz/50g, each approx 136yd/125m (cotton) 7 (7, 9, 10) balls in #60437 pink

■ One pair each size 10¹/₂ and 15 (7mm and 10mm) knitting needles OR SIZE TO OBTAIN GAUGE

■ Six ³/₄"/20mm buttons

■ Stitch holders

SIZES

Sized for Small (Medium, Large, X-Large). Shown in size Medium.

FINISHED MEASUREMENTS

■ Bust (buttoned) 33 (36, 38, 41)"/83.5 (91.5, 96.5, 104)cm

■ Length 19¹/₄ (19³/₄, 20¹/₄, 20³/₄)"/49 (50, 51.5, 52.5)cm

■ Upper arm 13 (14, 14¹/₂, 15¹/₄)"/33 (35.5, 37, 39)cm

GAUGE

11 sts and 14 rows to 4"/10cm over St st using 3 strands of yarn and larger needles.
TAKE TIME TO CHECK YOUR GAUGE.

BACK

With smaller needles and 3 strands of yarn, cast on 46 (50, 54, 58) sts.
Row 1 (RS) K2, *p2, k2; rep from * to end.
Row 2 K1 (selvage st), p1, *k2, p2; rep from * end last rep p1, k1 (selvage st). Rep rows 1 and 2 for rib twice more. K next RS rows. Change to larger needles and k next WS row, inc 1 (2, 0, 0) sts—47 (52, 54, 58) sts. Work even in St st (with k1 selvage sts each side of row) until piece measures 11¹/₂"/29cm from beg.

Armhole shaping
Bind off 3 sts at beg of next 2 rows.
Next row (RS) K1, SKP, k to last 3 sts, k2tog, k1.

Next row K1, p to last st, k1. Rep last 2 rows 1 (2, 2, 3) times more—37 (40, 42, 44) sts. Work even (with selvage sts) until armhole measures 7 (7¹/₂, 8, 8¹/₂)"/18 (19, 20.5, 21.5)cm.

Shoulder shaping
Bind off 5 (5, 6, 6) sts at beg of next 2 rows, 5 (6, 6, 6) sts at beg of next 2 rows. Bind off rem 17 (18, 18, 20) sts for back neck.

LEFT FRONT

With smaller needles and 3 strands of yarn, cast on 26 (30, 30, 34) sts. Rep rows 1 and 2 of back 3 times.
Next row (RS) K20 (24, 24, 28) sts inc 2 (0, 2, 0) sts evenly, sl last 6 sts to a holder to be worked later for band—22 (24, 26, 28) sts rem. Change to larger needles and k next WS row. Then cont in St st (with k1 selvage sts each side) until piece measures 11¹/₂"/29cm from beg.

Armhole shaping
Next row (RS) Bind off 3 sts, work to end. Work 1 row even.
Next row (RS) K1, SKP, k to end. Work 1 row even. Rep last 2 rows 1 (2, 2, 3) times more—17 (18, 20, 21) sts. Work even until armhole measures 2¹/₂ (3, 3¹/₂, 4)"/6.5 (7.5, 9, 10)cm.

Neck shaping
Next row (RS) K to last 2 sts, k2tog. Cont to dec 1 st at neck edge every row 4 (4, 5, 8) times more, every other row 2 (2, 2, 0) times—10 (11, 12, 12)

sts rem. Place a yarn marker at neck edge on last dec row. Work even until armhole measures same as back. Shape shoulder as on back.

RIGHT FRONT

Work to correspond to left front, reversing shaping and having 6-st band at beg of RS rows and working one yo, p2tog buttonhole in center of band when piece measures ¹/₂"/1.25cm from beg.

SLEEVES

With smaller needles and 3 strands of yarn, cast on 22 (22, 22, 26) sts. Work in rib and garter ridge as on back for 2"/5cm changing to larger needles on 2nd row. Then cont in St st, inc 1 st each side every 4th row 8 (9, 10, 9) times—38 (40, 42, 44) sts. Work even in St st until piece measures 17"/43cm from beg.

Cap shaping
Bind off 3 sts at beg of next 2 rows, 2 sts at beg of next 4 rows, dec 1 st each side every other row 4 (5, 6, 7) times—16 sts. Bind off.

FINISHING

Block pieces lightly to measurements. With smaller needles, work in rib across 6 sts of left front band, inc 1 st at inside edges for selvage st. Work in rib on 7 sts until band fits along center front edges, then along neck shaping to marker, stretching lightly to fit. Bind off. Place

(Continued on page 135)

Mesh Marvel

for intermediate knitters

Spring and summer are the times of the year to get a bit revealing, and this mesh pullover from Norah Gaughan is a modest-yet-modish starting point. If you like a little more body to an openwork design, don't fret: stockinette-stitched panels on the sleeves keep this cool design from being just another beach cover-up. "Mesh Marvel" first appeared in the Spring/Summer '03 issue of *Family Circle Easy Knitting*.

MATERIALS
- ◼ *Cabaret* by Artful Yarns/JCA, 1³/₄oz/50g balls, each approx 78yd/72m (cotton)
  12 (13, 14, 15, 16) balls in #6152 butter yellow
- ◼ One pair size 9 (5.5mm) needles OR SIZE TO OBTAIN GAUGE

SIZES
Sized for Small (Medium, Large, X-Large, XX-Large). Shown in size Small.

FINISHED MEASUREMENTS
- ◼ Bust 38 (40, 44, 46, 49)"/97 (101, 111, 117, 125)cm
- ◼ Length 24 (24¹/₂, 24¹/₂, 25, 25¹/₂)"/61 (62, 62, 63.5, 65)cm
- ◼ Upper arm 14 (15, 16, 17, 18)"/36 (38, 41, 43, 46)cm

GAUGE
16 sts and 22 rows to 4"/10cm over lace pat st using size 9 (5.5mm) needles.
TAKE TIME TO CHECK YOUR GAUGE.

LACE PATTERN STITCH
(multiple of 6 sts plus 3)
Row 1 (RS) K2, yo, ssk, k1, *k2tog, yo, k1, yo, ssk, k1; rep from *, end k2tog, yo, k2.
Row 2 P3, *yo, p3tog, yo, p3; rep from * to end.
Row 3 K2, k2tog, yo, k1, *yo, ssk, k1, k2tog, yo, k1; rep from *, end yo, ssk, k2.
Row 4 P1, p2tog, yo, *p3, yo, p3tog, yo; rep from *, end p3, yo, p2tog, p1.
Rep rows 1-4 for lace pat st.

BACK
Cast on 75 (81, 87, 93, 99) sts. Purl 1 row on WS. Then work in lace pat st until piece measures 24 (24¹/₂, 24¹/₂, 25, 25¹/₂)"/61 (62, 62, 63.5, 65)cm from beg. Bind off loosely knitwise on a RS row.

FRONT
Work as for back.

SLEEVES
Cast on 45 (45, 51, 57, 57) sts. Purl 1 row on WS. Then work in lace pat st for 10 rows. **Inc row (RS)** K1, M1, work pat to last st, M1, k1. Cont to inc sts each side, working inc sts in St st; rep inc row every 8th row 8 (10, 10, 9, 7) times more, every 6th row 0 (0, 0, 0, 4) times—63 (67, 73, 77, 81) sts. Work even until piece measures 17"/43cm from beg. Bind off.

FINISHING
Block pieces lightly to measurements. Leaving the center 12"/30.5cm open for neck (or approx 48 center sts), sew shoulders tog on front and back for approx 3¹/₂ (4, 5, 5¹/₂, 6¹/₄)"/9 (10, 12.5, 14, 16)cm. Place markers at 7 (7¹/₂, 8, 8¹/₂, 9)"/18 (19, 20.5, 21.5, 23)cm down from shoulders. Sew sleeves to armholes between markers. Sew side and sleeve seams.

(Schematics on page 135)

Cropped Cut
for beginner knitters

Enjoy the cool evenings of spring and early summer with this relaxed pullover by Rosemary Drysdale. A quick knit in stockinette stitch, this sweater works by the poolside or in the countryside. "Cropped Cut" first appeared in the Spring/Summer '99 issue of *Family Circle Easy Knitting*.

MATERIALS

- *Goa* by GGH/Muench Yarns, 1³/₄oz/50g balls, each approx 66yd/ 60m (cotton) 25 (29, 31, 33, 37) balls in #113 blue
- Size 15 (10mm) needles OR SIZE TO OBTAIN GAUGE
- Size J/10 (6mm) crochet hook
- Stitch markers

SIZES

Sized for Small (Medium, Large, X-Large, XX-Large). Shown in size Medium.

FINISHED MEASUREMENTS

- Bust 40 (43, 46, 49, 52)"/101.5 (109, 117, 124.5, 132)cm
- Length 17 (17¹/₂, 18, 19, 19¹/₂)"/43 (44.5, 45.5, 48.5, 49.5)cm
- Upper arm 17 (18, 19, 20, 21)"/43 (45.5, 48, 50.5, 53)cm

GAUGE

8 sts and 12 rows to 4"/10cm over St st using size 15 (10mm) needles and 3 strands of yarn held tog.
TAKE TIME TO CHECK YOUR GAUGE.

Notes

1 Work with three strands of yarn held tog throughout.

2 K first and last st of every row for garter st selvage. These sts are not counted in the finished measurements.

BACK

With 3 strands of yarn held tog, cast on 42 (45, 48, 51, 54) sts. Work in St st and garter st selvages until piece measures 16 (16¹/₂, 17, 18, 18¹/₂)"/40.5 (42, 43, 46, 47)cm from beg, end with a WS row.

Neck shaping

Next row (RS) Work 15 (16, 17, 18, 20) sts, join a 2nd ball of yarn and bind off center 12 (13, 14, 15, 14) sts, work to end. Working both sides at once, bind off 2 sts from each neck edge once. Work even, if necessary, until piece measures 17 (17¹/₂, 18, 19, 19¹/₂)"/43 (44.5, 45.5, 48.5, 49.5)cm from beg. Bind off rem 13 (14, 15, 16, 18) sts each side for shoulders.

FRONT

Work as for back until piece measures 15 (15¹/₂, 16, 17, 17¹/₂)"/38 (39.5, 40.5, 43.5, 44.5)cm from beg, end with a WS row.

Neck shaping

Next row (RS) Work 16 (17, 18, 19, 21) sts, join a 2nd ball of yarn and bind off center 10 (11, 12, 13, 12) sts, work to end. Working both sides at once, bind off from each neck edge 2 sts once, 1 st once. Work even until piece measures same as back. Bind off rem 13 (14, 15, 16, 18) sts each side for shoulders.

SLEEVES

With 3 strands of yarn held tog, cast on 18 (18, 18, 20, 20) sts. Work in St st, inc 1 st each side every 4th row 3 (5, 8, 7, 10) times, every 6th row 6 (5, 3, 4, 2) times—36 (38, 40, 42, 44) sts. Work even until piece measures 17¹/₂ (18, 18, 18¹/₂, 18¹/₂)"/44.5 (45.5, 45.5, 47, 47)cm from beg. Bind off.

FINISHING

Block pieces to measurements. Sew shoulder seams. Place markers 8¹/₂ (9, 9¹/₂, 10, 10¹/₂)"/ 21.5 (23, 24, 25.5, 26.5)cm down from shoulders on front and back. Sew top of sleeves between markers. Sew side and sleeve seams. With RS facing, crochet hook and 3 strands of yarn held tog, work 1 row of sc evenly around neck. Fasten off.

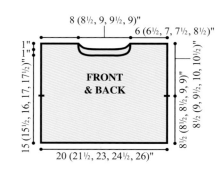

8 (8¹/₂, 9, 9¹/₂, 9)"
6 (6¹/₂, 7, 7¹/₂, 8¹/₂)"
1"
1"
FRONT & BACK
15 (15¹/₂, 16, 17, 17¹/₂)"
8¹/₂ (9, 9¹/₂, 9)"
8¹/₂ (9, 9¹/₂, 10, 10¹/₂)"
20 (21¹/₂, 23, 24¹/₂, 26)"

17 (18, 19, 20, 21)"
SLEEVE
17¹/₂ (18, 18, 18¹/₂, 18¹/₂)"
8 (8, 8, 9, 9)"

Fiestawear

for beginner knitters

Make a run for the border in this nifty pullover designed by Charlotte Parry. Details such as embroidered flower ribbon, flirty fringe and sassy tassels add a touch of ethnicity and a whole lot of originality. "Fiestawear" first appeared in the Spring/Summer '03 issue of *Family Circle Easy Knitting*.

MATERIALS

- *1824 Cotton* by Mission Falls/Unique Kolours, 1³/₄oz/50g balls, each approx 84yd/77m (cotton) 11 (11, 12, 14, 15) balls in #102 ecru
- One pair each sizes 8 and 9 (5 and 5.5mm) needles or size to obtain gauge
- Size G/6 (4.5mm) crochet hook
- 2yd/2m of black fringe #0821 and 4yd/4m of floral ribbon #5109 by Mokuba
- Purchased black tassels and 1yd/1m black twisted cord

SIZES

Sized for Small (Medium, Large, X-Large, XX-Large). Shown in size Medium.

FINISHED MEASUREMENTS

- Bust 40 (44, 47, 50, 53)"/101.5 (111.5, 119.5, 127, 134.5)cm
- Length 23 (23¹/₂, 24, 24¹/₂, 25)"/58.5 (59.5, 61, 62, 63.5)cm (without fringe)
- Upper arm 12¹/₂ (13¹/₂, 15, 16, 17)"/32 (34, 38, 40.5, 43)cm

GAUGE

17 sts and 24 rows to 4"/10cm over St st using larger needles.
TAKE TIME TO CHECK YOUR GAUGE.

BACK

With larger needles, cast on 84 (94, 100, 106, 114) sts. Work in St st for 14"/35.5cm.

Raglan armhole shaping

Bind off 4 (5, 5, 5, 6) sts at beg of next 2 rows. Dec 1 st each side every 4th row 5 (4, 3, 2, 0) times, every other row 13 (17, 20, 24, 29) times. Bind off rem 42 (42, 44, 44 44) sts for back neck.

FRONT

Work as for back until piece measures 14¹/₂ (15, 15¹/₂, 16, 16¹/₂)"/37 (38, 39.5, 40.5, 42)cm from beg. Mark center of piece.

Divide for placket

Cont armhole shaping, work to center, join a 2nd ball of yarn, work to end. Working both sides at once, work even until armhole measures 5¹/₂ (6, 6¹/₂, 7, 7¹/₂)"/14 (15, 16.5, 17.5, 19)cm.

Neck shaping

Cont armhole shaping and bind off at each neck edge 8 (8, 9, 9, 9) sts once, 3 sts twice, 2 sts 3 times, 1 st once.

SLEEVES

Cast on 36 (36, 36, 38, 38) sts. Work in St st, inc 1 st each side every 8th (6th, 6th, 6th, 6th) row 6 (5, 12, 10, 8) times, every 10th (8th, 4th, 4th, 4th) row 3 (6, 2, 5, 9) times—54 (58, 64, 68, 72) sts. Work even until piece measures 14"/35.5cm from beg.

Cap shaping

Bind off 4 (5, 5, 5, 6) sts at beg of next 2 rows, dec 1 st each side every 4th row 4 (5, 3, 3, 3) times, then every other row 15 (15, 20, 22, 23) times. Bind off rem 8 sts.

FINISHING

Block pieces to measurements. Sew shoulder seams.

Neckband casing

With RS facing and smaller needles, pick up and k 118 (118, 122, 122, 122) sts evenly around neck edge. Beg with a WS row, work 2 rows in St st. K next row on WS for turning ridge. Work 2 rows more in St st. Bind off. Fold to inside at turning ridge and sew in place. Set in sleeves. Sew side and sleeve seams. Thread twisted cord through neckband. Adjust to desired length, Attach a tassel to each end.

Lower edgings

Beg at center back, place fringe along lower edge of body and pin or baste in place. Beg at center back, place ribbon over fringe, covering edges. Using a running st, sew ribbon and fringe in place at lower edge through all thicknesses. Sew top edge of ribbon in place. Fold ends under at center back to neaten and sew in place.

Work in same way along lower edge of each sleeve.

Neck edging

Beg at center back neck, pin or base ribbon along neck just below neckband casing, to center front opening, fold ribbon for mitered edge to fit corner, cont down to ¹/₂"/1.5cm below beg of placket opening, fold ribbon to make a point and cont up the opposite side and fold for mitered edge to fit 2nd corner, cont around to center back neck. Fold end under to neaten. Using a running st, sew top and bottom edges in place.

(Schematics on page 135)

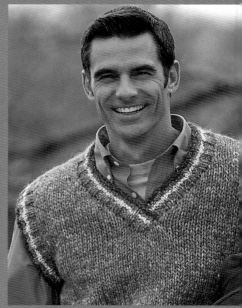

His 'n Hers

Make it a match in fashions for him and her.

The Two of Us
for intermediate knitters

Easy-fitting classics like these designs by Mari Lynn Patrick make a weekend getaway to the country extra special. His rugged vest looks dapper in a muted heather blue with striped edges. Her striped sweater boasts bold ribs for maximum style and comfort. "The Two of Us" first appeared in the Fall '00 issue of *Family Circle Easy Knitting*.

MATERIALS

- *Soho Bulky Tweed* by Tahki Yarns/Tahki•Stacy Charles Inc., 3¹⁄₂oz/100g balls, each approx 110yd/100m (wool)

Women's sweater
- 1 (1, 2, 2) balls each in #301 ecru (A)
- 2 (2, 3, 3) balls each in #316 brown (B), #327 olive (D), #317 blue (E) and #326 burgundy (F)
- 1 ball in #304 charcoal (C)
- One pair each sizes 10¹⁄₂ and 11 (6.5 and 8mm) needles OR SIZE TO OBTAIN GAUGE
- Stitch holders

Men's vest
- 5 (5, 6, 6, 6) balls in #317 lt blue (MC)
- 1 ball each in #304 charcoal (A) and #301 ecru (B)
- One pair each sizes 10 and 11 (6 and 8mm) OR SIZE TO OBTAIN GAUGE
- Size 10 (6mm) circular needle, 16"/40cm long

SIZES

Women's Pullover
Sized for Small (Medium, Large, X-Large). Shown in size Medium.

Men's vest
Sized for Man's Small (Medium, Large, X-Large, XX-Large). Shown in size Large.

WOMEN'S VERSION

FINISHED MEASUREMENTS

- Bust 35 (38, 41, 44)"/89 (96.5, 104, 111.5)cm
- Length 22 (22¹⁄₂, 23, 23¹⁄₂)"/56 (57, 58.5, 59.5)cm
- Upper arm 14¹⁄₂ (15, 16, 17)"/37 (38, 40.5, 43)cm

GAUGE

14 sts and 15 rows to 4"/10cm over k3, p2 rib using larger needles.
TAKE TIME TO CHECK YOUR GAUGE.

RIB PATTERN

Row 1 (RS) P2, *k3, p2; rep from * to end.

Row 2 K the knit and p the purl sts.
Rep row 2 for rib pat.

STRIPE PATTERN

*Work 1 row in k3, p2 rib with A. P 1 row with B, work 7 rows in k3, p2 rib with B. P 1 row with C, work 1 row in k3, p2 rib with C. P 1 row with D, work 7 rows in k3, p2 rib with D. P 1 row with C, work 1 row in k3, p2 rib with C. P 1 row with E, work 7 rows in rib with E. P 1 row with A, work 1 row in rib with A. P 1 row with F, work 7 rows in rib with F. P 1 row with A. Rep from * (40 rows) for stripe pat.

BACK

With larger needles and A, cast on 62 (67, 72, 77) sts. Work in rib and stripe pat until piece measures 13¹⁄₂"/34cm from beg.

Armhole shaping

Bind off 3 (3, 4, 4) sts at beg of next 2 rows, 2 sts at beg of next 2 rows, dec 1 st each side of next row then every other row 3 (3, 3, 4) times more—44 (49, 52, 55) sts. Work even until armhole measures 7¹⁄₂ (8, 8¹⁄₂, 9)"/19 (20.5, 21.5, 23)cm.

Shoulder and neck shaping

Bind off 5 (6, 6, 7) sts at beg of next 2 rows, 5 (6, 7, 7) sts at beg of next 2 rows. Sl center 24 (25, 26, 27) sts to a holder for neck.

FRONT

Work as for back until armhole measures 3 (3¹⁄₂, 4, 4¹⁄₂)"/7.5 (9, 10, 11.5)cm.

Neck shaping

Next row (RS) Sl center 10 (11, 12, 13) sts, to a holder, join 2nd ball of yarn and work to end. Working both sides at once, bind off 2 sts from each neck edge twice, dec 1 st each side every other row 3 times—10 (12, 13, 14) sts rem each side. When same length as back, shape shoulders as for back.

SLEEVES

Note Read before beg to knit.
With larger needles and A, cast on 32 sts. For stripe pat work 1 row in k3, p2 rib with A. P 1

(Continued on page 136)

Man's Best Friend

for beginner knitters

A solid style basic for any man's closet and just the thing for a brisk autumn day, this simple V-neck from Norah Gaughan works up easily. A little ribbing down the front gives it a contemporary edge. "Man's Best Friend" first appeared in the Fall '99 issue of *Family Circle Easy Knitting*.

MATERIALS

- *Galway* by Plymouth Yarns, 3¹/₂oz/100g balls each approx 210yd/193m (wool)
  9 (9, 10, 11, 12) balls in #556 royal
- One pair each sizes 10 and 11 (6 and 8mm) needles OR SIZE TO OBTAIN GAUGE
- Size 10 (6mm) circular needle, 24"/60cm long

SIZES

Sized for Man's Small (Medium, Large, X-Large, XX-Large). Shown in size X-Large.

FINISHED MEASUREMENTS

- Chest 48 (50, 52, 55, 57)"/122 (127, 132, 139.5, 144.5)cm
- Length 25¹/₂ (26, 26, 26¹/₂, 27)"/64.5 (66, 66, 67, 68.5)cm
- Upper arm 20¹/₂ (21, 21, 22¹/₂, 23¹/₂)"/52 (53, 53, 57, 59.5)cm

GAUGE

11 sts and 17 rows to 4"/10cm over St st using a double strand of yarn and larger needles. TAKE TIME TO CHECK YOUR GAUGE.

Notes

1 Work with a double strand of yarn throughout.

2 Due to the seaming for this extra bulky style, finished measurements reflect sewn pieces, not exact schematic pieces.

BACK

With smaller needles and a double strand of yarn, cast on 68 (70, 74, 78, 80) sts. Work in k1, p1 rib for 2"/5cm, end with a RS row. Change to larger needles and work in St st (beg with a p row) until piece measures 25¹/₂ (26, 26, 26¹/₂, 27)"/64.5 (66, 66, 67, 68.5)cm from beg. Bind off.

FRONT

With smaller needles and a double strand of yarn, cast on 68 (70, 74, 78, 80) sts. Work in k1, p1 rib for 2"/5cm, end with a RS row. Change to larger needles. **Next row (WS)** P30 (31, 33, 35, 36), k2, p1, k2, p1, k2, p to end. **Next row (RS)** K30 (31, 33, 35, 36), p2, sl 1 purlwise wyib, k2, sl 1 purlwise wyib, p2, k to end. Rep last 2 rows for pat until piece measures 18 (18¹/₂, 18¹/₂, 19, 19¹/₂)"/45.5 (47, 47, 48, 49.5)cm from beg.

Neck shaping

Next row (RS) K32 (33, 35, 37, 38), join another double strand of yarn and bind off center 4 sts, work to end. Working both sides at once, dec 1 st each side of neck edge every other row 10 (12, 12, 14, 14) times, every 4th row 2 (1, 1, 0, 0) times. Work even on 20 (20, 22, 23, 24) sts each side until same length as back. Bind off rem sts each side for shoulders.

SLEEVES

With smaller needles and a double strand of yarn, cast on 30 (32, 32, 34, 34) sts. Work in k1, p1 rib for 2"/5cm. Change to larger needles and work in St st, inc 1 st each side every 4th row 10 (10, 10, 13, 16) times, every 6th row 4 (4, 4, 2, 0) times—58 (60, 60, 64, 66) sts. Work even until piece measures 19"/48cm from beg. Bind off.

FINISHING

Block pieces to measurements. Sew shoulder seams.

Neckband

With circular needle and a double strand of yarn, beg at left of 4-st center bind-off, pick up and k 82 (86, 86, 90, 90) sts evenly around neck edge, ending at right of 4-st center bind off. Working back and forth in rows, work in k1, p1 rib for 1¹/₄"/3cm. Bind off in rib. Sew ends of rib at center V-neck edge, overlapping left over right neck edge. Fold sleeves in half and sew into armholes. Sew side and sleeve seams.

(Schematics on page 137)

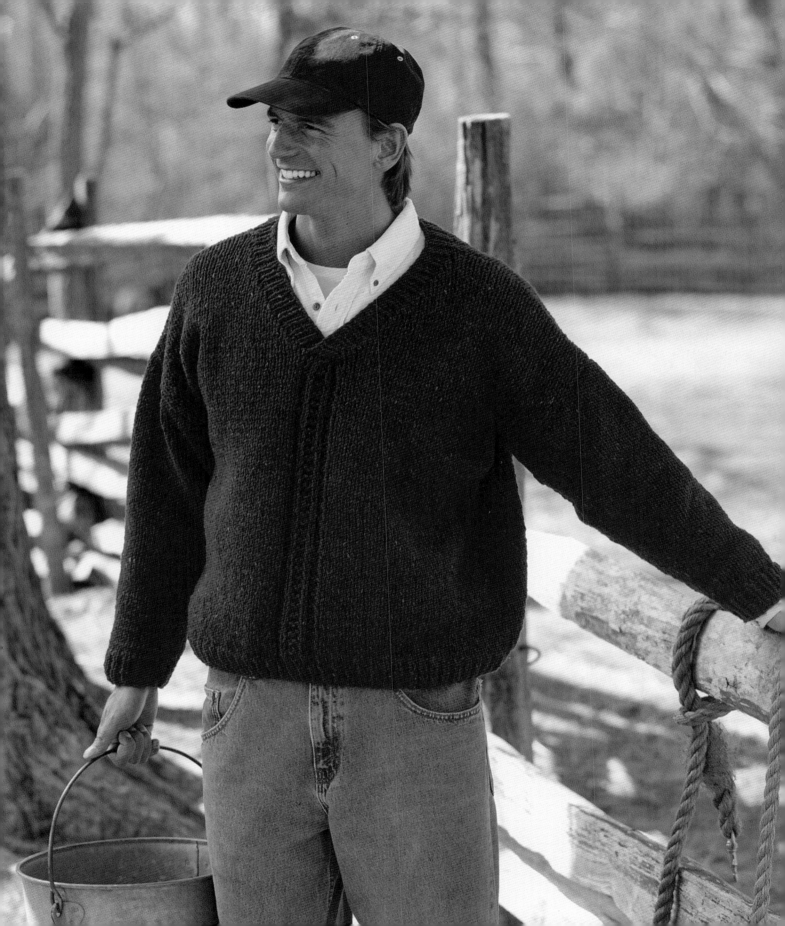

The Natural

for beginner knitters

Whether it's a walk in the Berkshires or a picnic in Central Park, this split-neck pullover from Betsy Westman is a natural for a day out. Textured ribbing and variegated yarn add depth, while crocheted edging makes for a polished finish. "The Natural" first appeared in the Fall '00 issue of *Family Circle Easy Knitting*.

MATERIALS

- *14-Ply* by Wool Pak Yarns NZ/Baabajoes Wool Co., 8oz/250g, each approx 310yd/286m (wool)
  3 (3, 4, 4) hanks in heather
- One pair each sizes 10 and 11 (6 and 8mm) needles OR SIZE TO OBTAIN GAUGE
- Size 10 (6mm) circular needle, 16"/40cm long
- Size J/10 (6mm) crochet

SIZES

Sized for Men's Small (Medium, Large, X-Large). Shown in size Medium.

FINISHED MEASUREMENTS

- Chest 42 (47, 51, 56)"/106.5 (119, 129.5, 142)cm
- Length 28 (29, 29, 30)"/71 (73.5, 73.5, 76)cm
- Upper arm 20 (21½, 21½, 22)"/51 (54.5, 54.5, 56)cm

GAUGE

12 sts and 16 rows to 4"/10cm over chart pat using larger needles.
TAKE TIME TO CHECK YOUR GAUGE.

BACK

With smaller needles, cast on 63 (70, 77, 84) sts.
Row 1 (RS) *K4, p3; rep from * to end. **Row 2** K the knit and p the purl sts. Rep row 2 for k4, p3 rib until piece measures 2½"/6.5cm from beg. Change to larger needles.

Beg chart pat

Row 1 (RS) Beg with st 1 (4, 2, 1), work 5-st rep (sts 4 to 8) 12 (14, 15, 16) times, end with st 8 (8, 8, 9). Cont in pat as established until piece measures 17 (17½, 17½, 18)"/43 (44.5, 44.5, 45.5)cm from beg.

Armhole shaping

Bind off 2 sts at beg of next 2 rows. Dec 1 st each side of next row then every other row 1 (1, 2, 2) times more—55 (62, 67, 74) sts. Work even until armhole measures 10 (10½, 10½, 11)"/25.5 (26.5, 26.5, 28)cm.

Neck and shoulder shaping

Bind off 7 (8, 9, 11) sts at beg of next 2 rows, 7 (9, 10, 11) sts at beg of next 2 rows, AT SAME TIME, bind off center 21 (22, 23, 24) sts and working both sides at once, bind off 3 sts from each neck edge once.

FRONT

Work as for back until armhole measures 7 (7½, 7½, 8)"/18 (19, 19, 20.5)cm.

Neck split

Next row (RS) Work 27 (31, 33, 37) sts, join 2nd ball of yarn and bind off 1 (0, 1, 0) st, work to end. Working both sides at once, work 1 row even.

Neck shaping

Next row (RS) Work to last 2 sts of first side, k2tog; on second side, k2tog, work to end. Work 2 rows even. Bind off 5 (6, 6, 7) sts from each neck edge once, 4 sts once, 2 sts once and 1 st once—14 (17, 19, 22) sts each side. When same length as back, shape shoulders as for back.

SLEEVES

With smaller needles, cast on 30 sts. **Row 1 (RS)** K3, *p3, k4; rep from * end last rep k3. **Row 2** K the knit and p the purl sts. Rep row 2 for k4, p3 rib until piece measures 2½"/6.5cm from beg, inc 2 sts on last WS row—32 sts. Change to larger needles.

Beg chart pat

Row 1 (RS) Beg with st 2, work 5-st rep 6 times. Cont in pat as established, inc 1 st each side (working inc sts into pat) every 4th row 14 (16, 16, 17) times—60 (64, 64, 66) sts. Work even until piece measures 20 (20, 21, 22)"/51 (51, 53, 56)cm from beg.

Cap shaping

Bind off 2 sts at beg of next 2 rows, 1 st at beg of next 4 rows—52 (56, 56, 58) sts. Bind off.

FINISHING

Block pieces to measurements. Sew shoulder seams.

Neckband

With RS facing and circular needle, beg at neck shaping above neck split, pick up and k 74 (74, 78, 78) sts evenly around neck edge. Work back and forth in k2, p2 rib for 1"/2.5cm. Bind off in rib. With crochet hook, work an edge of sc around the center V-opening. Sew sleeves into armholes. Sew side and sleeve seams.

(Schematics on page 137)

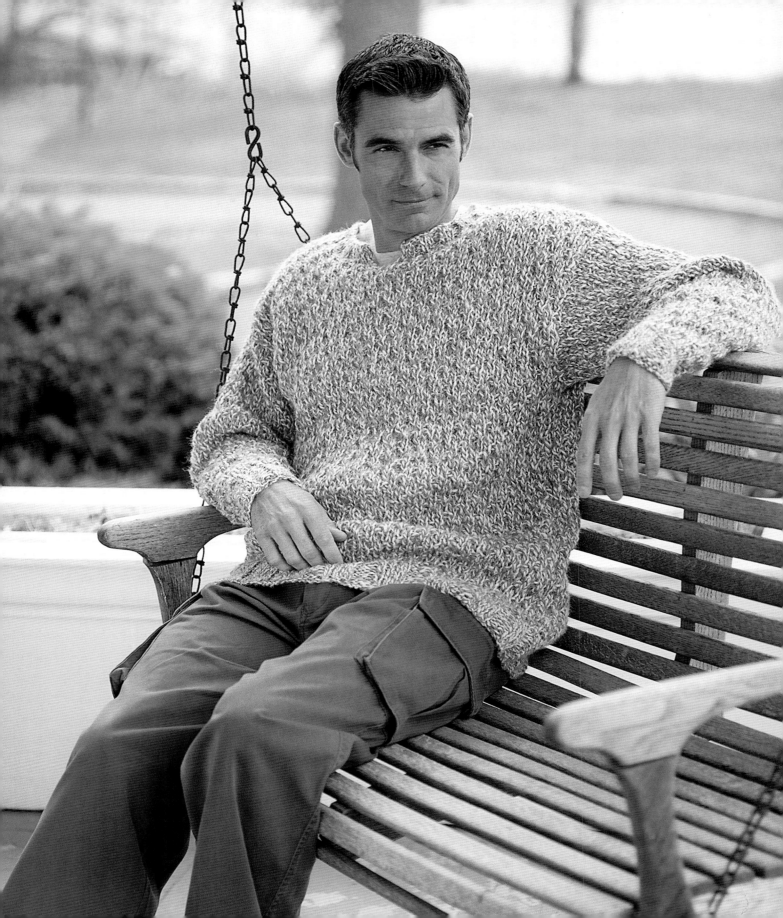

Sporty Stripes

for beginner knitters

This his-and-hers pullover set designed by Susan Mills is a sporty alternative for a crisp autumn day on the golf course or the front porch. Wide ribbing marks the cuffs of his, while hers goes without for a lighter touch. "Sporty Stripes" first appeared in the Fall '00 issue of *Family Circle Easy Knitting*.

MATERIALS

▨ *Lite-Lopi* by Reynolds/JCA, 1¾oz/50g balls, each approx 109yd/100m (wool)

Women's version

   1 (2, 2, 2, 3) balls in #432 grape heather (A), 3 (3, 4, 4, 4) balls in #419 ocean (B)

   3 (3, 3, 4, 4) balls in #418 blue heather (C), 2 (3, 3, 3, 4) balls in #422 sage heather (D)

   1 (2, 2, 2, 3) balls in #421 celery heather (E), 1 ball in #420 gold heather (F)

▨ One pair size 10 (6mm) needles OR SIZE TO OBTAIN GAUGE

Men's version

   2 (2, 3, 3, 4) balls in #432 grape heather (A), 4 (4, 5, 5, 6) balls in #419 ocean (B)

   4 (4, 4, 5, 5) balls in #418 blue heather (C), 3 (3, 4, 4, 4) balls in #422 sage heather (D)

   2 (2, 2, 2, 3) balls in #421 celery heather (E), 1 ball in #426 gold heather (F)

▨ One pair each sizes 8 and 10 (5 and 6mm) needles OR SIZE TO OBTAIN GAUGE

▨ Size 8 (5mm) circular needle, 16"/40cm long

SIZES

Women's Version

Sized for Small (Medium, Large, X-Large, XX-Large). Shown in size Medium.

Men's Version

Sized for Men's Small (Medium, Large, X-Large, XX-Large). Shown in size Large.

WOMEN'S VERSION

FINISHED MEASUREMENTS

▨ Bust 36 (40, 44, 48, 52)"/91.5 (101.5, 111.5, 122, 132)cm

▨ Length 21 (22, 22, 23, 24)"/53.5 (55.5, 55.5, 58.5, 61)cm

▨ Upper arm 18 (19½, 19½, 20, 20)"/46 (49, 49, 51, 51)cm

GAUGE

12 sts and 18 rows to 4"/10cm over St st using 2 strands of yarn held tog and size 10 (6mm) needles.

TAKE TIME TO CHECK YOUR GAUGE.

STRIPE PATTERN

Working with 2 strands of yarn, work *2 rows with D and E, 2 rows with E and F, 2 rows with D and E, 4 rows with C and D, 4 rows with B and C, 6 rows with A and B, 4 rows with B and C, 4 rows with C and D; rep from * (28 rows) for stripe pat.

BACK

With 1 strand each D and E, cast on 54 (60, 66, 72, 78) sts. Work in St st and stripe pat until piece measures 20 (21, 21, 22, 23)"/51 (53, 53, 56, 58.5)cm from beg.

Neck and shoulder shaping

Bind off 7 (9, 9, 11, 12) sts at beg of next 2 rows, 8 (9, 10, 11, 13) sts at beg of next 2 rows, AT SAME TIME, bind off center 22 (22, 26, 26, 26) sts and working both sides at once, dec 1 st from each neck edge once.

FRONT

Work as for back until piece measures 13 (14, 13½, 14, 15)"/33 (35.5, 34, 35.5, 38)cm from beg.

V-neck shaping

Next row (RS) Work 27 (30, 33, 36, 39) sts, join another 2 strands of yarn and work to end. Working both sides at once, work 1 row even.

Dec row (RS) Work to last 4 sts on first side, k2tog, k2; on second side, k2, ssk, work to end. Rep dec row every other row 10 (10, 12, 11, 11) times more, every 4th row 1 (1, 1, 2, 2) times—

15 (18, 19, 22, 25) sts rem each side. When same length as back, shape shoulders as on back.

SLEEVES

With 1 strand each D and E, cast on 30 sts. Work in St st and stripe pat, inc 1 st each side every 4th row 0 (2, 2, 8, 8) times, every 6th row 10 (12, 12, 7, 7) times, every 8th row 2 (0, 0, 0, 0) times—54 (58, 58, 60, 60) sts. Work even until piece measures 21 (21, 21, 20, 20)"/53 (53, 53, 51, 51)cm from beg. Bind off.

FINISHING

Block pieces to measurements. Sew shoulder seams. Place markers at 9 (9¾, 9¾, 10, 10)"/23 (24.5, 24.5, 25.5, 25.5)cm down from shoulders. Sew sleeves to armholes between markers. Sew side and sleeve seams.

MEN'S VERSION

FINISHED MEASUREMENTS

▨ Chest 40 (44, 48, 52, 56)"/101.5 (111.5, 122, 132, 142)cm

▨ Length 24½ (24½, 25½, 25½, 26½)"/62 (62, 65, 65, 67)cm

▨ Upper arm 20 (20, 21½, 21½, 22)"/51 (51, 54, 54, 56)cm

(Continued on page 138)

Plus-Size Knits Basics

Nothing is more rewarding than knitting a sweater for yourself and the ones you love. In *Family Circle Plus-Size Knits*, we offer a gamut of figure-flattering styles. From easy weekend projects like the "Stripe it Up" vest to more complex patterns such as "My Fair Lady," this collection accommodates every skill level from novice to expert.

Packed with more than fifty knit and crochet projects, this book features contemporary styles for plus-sized figures in updated yarns. However, feel free to explore your more creative side—we encourage it! Surprisingly wonderful effects can be achieved by simply substituting the yarn or changing the color.

Whether you are searching for a casual everyday pullover, an exquisite evening shawl or even a rugged vest for your man, you'll find the perfect pattern in this assortment.

GARMENT CONSTRUCTION

Even though most of the garments in this book are made in pieces, if you are a fairly experienced knitter, you can try knitting many of them in the round, or pick up your sleeve stitches at the shoulder seams and work down to the cuff. You just need to make some simple adjustments to the pattern.

SIZING

Since clothing measurements have changed in recent decades, it is important to measure yourself carefully to determine which size is best for you.

YARN SELECTION

For an exact reproduction of the projects photographed, use the yarn listed in the "Materials" section of the pattern. We've chosen yarns that are readily available in the U.S. and Canada at the time of printing. The Resources guide on page 143 provides addresses of yarn distributors. Contact them for the name of a retailer in your area.

YARN SUBSTITUTION

If you want to work with a different yarn, by all means do so. Perhaps you view small-scale projects as a chance to incorporate leftovers from your stash, or the yarn specified may not be available in your area. You'll need to knit to the given gauge to obtain the knitted measurements with a substitute yarn (see "Gauge" below). Be sure to consider how the fiber content of the substitute yarn will affect the comfort and the ease of care of your projects.

After you've successfully gauge-swatched a substitute yarn, you'll need to figure out how much of the new yarn the project requires. First, find the total length of the original yarn in the pattern (multiply number of balls by yards/meters per ball). Divide this figure by the new yards/meters per ball (listed on the ball band). Round up to the next whole number. The answer is the number of balls required.

FOLLOWING CHARTS

Charts are a convenient way to follow colorwork, lace, cable, and other stitch patterns at a glance. *FCEK* stitch charts utilize the universal knitting language of "symbolcraft." When knitting back and forth in rows, read charts from right to left on right side (RS) rows and from left to right on wrong side (WS) rows, repeating any stitch and row repeats as directed in the pattern. When knitting in the round, read charts from right to left on every round. Posting a self-adhesive note under your working row is an easy way to keep track of your place on a chart.

LACE

Lace knitting provides a feminine touch. Knitted lace is formed with "yarn overs," which create an eyelet hole in combination with decreases that create directional effects. To make a yarn over (yo), merely pass the yarn over the right-hand needle to form a new loop. Decreases are worked as k2tog, ssk, or SKP depending on the desired slant and are spelled out specifically with each instruction. On the row or round that follows the lace or eyelet detail, each yarn over is treated as one stitch. If you're new to lace knitting, it's a good idea to count the stitches at the end of each row or round. Making a gauge swatch in the stitch pattern enables you to practice the lace pattern. Instead of binding off the swatch, place the final row on a holder, as the bind off tends to pull in the stitches and distort the gauge.

COLORWORK KNITTING

Two main types of colorwork are explored in this book.

GAUGE

It is still important to knit a gauge swatch to assure a perfect fit in a sweater. If the gauge is incorrect, a colorwork pattern may become distorted. The type of needles used—straight, circular, wood or metal—will influence gauge, so knit your swatch with the needles you plan to use for the project. Measure gauge as illustrated here. (Launder and block your gauge swatch before taking measurements). Try different needle sizes until your sample measures the required number of stitches and rows. To get fewer stitches to the inch/cm, use larger needles; to get more stitches to the inch/cm, use smaller needles. It's a good idea to keep your gauge swatch to test any embroidery or embellishment, as well as blocking and cleaning methods.

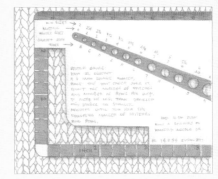

INTARSIA

Intarsia is accomplished with separate bobbins of individual colors. This method is ideal for large blocks of color or for motifs that aren't repeated close together. When changing colors, always pick up the new color and wrap it around the old color to prevent holes.

STRANDING

When motifs are closely placed, colorwork is accomplished by stranding along two or more colors per row, creating "floats" on the wrong side of the fabric. This technique is sometimes called Fair Isle knitting after the traditional Fair Isle patterns that are composed of small motifs with frequent color changes.

To keep an even tension and prevent holes while knitting, pick up yarns alternately over and under one another across or around. While knitting, stretch the stitches on the needle slightly wider than the length of the float at the back to keep work from puckering.

When changing colors at the beginning of rows or rounds, carry yarn along for a few rows only, or cut yarn and rejoin when needed. It is important to keep the "floats" small and neat so they don't catch when pulling on the piece.

BLOCKING

Blocking is an all-important finishing step in the knitting process. It is the best way to shape pattern pieces and smooth knitted edges in preparation for sewing together. Most garments retain their shape if the blocking stages in the instructions are followed carefully. Choose a blocking method according to the yarn care label and when in doubt, test-block your gauge swatch.

WET BLOCK METHOD

Using rust-proof pins, pin pieces to measurements on a flat surface and lightly dampen using a spray bottle. Allow to dry before removing pins.

STEAM BLOCK METHOD

With WS facing, pin pieces. Steam lightly, holding the iron 2"/5cm above the knitting. Do not press or it will flatten stitches.

FINISHING

The pieces in this book use a variety of finishing techniques. Directions for making fringes are on page 114. Also refer to the illustrations such as "To Begin Seaming" and "Invisible Seaming: Stockinette St" provided for other useful techniques.

HAND-SEWING

Several items in this book require hand-sewing in the finishing. Use a fine point hand sewing

needle and sewing thread that matches the color of the trim. Cut the unsewn ends at an angle to prevent unraveling. When sewing on a trim, use back stitch and keep the stitches small and even.

CARE

Refer to the yarn label for the recommended cleaning method. Many of the projects in the book can be either washed by hand, or in the machine on a gentle or wool cycle, in lukewarm water with a mild detergent. Do not agitate, or soak for more than 10 minutes. Rinse gently with tepid water, then fold in a towel and gently press the water out. Lay flat to dry away from excess heat and light. Check the yarn band for any specific care instructions such as dry cleaning or tumble drying.

TO BEGIN SEAMING

If you have left a long tail from your cast-on row, you can use this strand to begin sewing. To make a neat join at the lower edge with no gap, use the technique shown here. Thread the strand into a yarn needle. With the right sides of both pieces facing you, insert the yarn needle from back to front into the corner stitch of the piece without the tail. Making a figure eight with the yarn, insert the needle from back to front into the stitch with the cast-on tail. Tighten to close the gap.

INVISIBLE SEAMING: STOCKINETTE ST

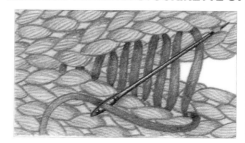

To make an invisible side seam in a garment worked in stockinette stitch, insert the tapestry needle under the horizontal bar between the first and second stitches. Insert the needle into the corresponding bar on the other piece. Pull the yarn gently until the sides meet. Continue alternating from side to side.

BASIC STITCHES

GARTER STITCH

Knit every row. Circular knitting: knit one round, then purl one round.

STOCKINETTE STITCH

Knit right-side rows and purl wrong-side rows. Circular knitting: knit all rounds. (UK: stocking stitch)

REVERSE STOCKINETTE STITCH

Purl right-side rows and knit wrong-side rows. Circular knitting: purl all rounds. (UK: reverse stocking stitch)

DUPLICATE STITCH

Duplicate stitch covers a knit stitch. Bring the needle up below the stitch to be worked. Insert the needle under both loops one row above and pull it through. Insert it back into the stitch below and through the center of the next stitch in one motion, as shown.

WORKING A YARN OVER

There are different ways to make a yarn over. Which method to use depends on where you are in the stitch pattern. If you do not make the yarn over in the right way, you may lose it on the following row, or make a yarn over that is too big. Here are the different variations:

Between two knit stitches: Bring the yarn from the back of the work to the front between the two needles. Knit the next stitch, bringing the yarn to the back over the right-hand needle, as shown.

Between a knit and a purl stitch: Bring the yarn from the back to the front between the two needles. Then bring it to the back over the right-hand needle and back to the front again, as shown. Purl the next stitch.

Between a purl and a knit stitch: Leave the yarn at the front of the work. Knit the next stitch, bringing the yarn to the back over the right-hand needle, as shown.

Between two purl stitches: Leave the yarn at the front of the work. Bring the yarn to the back over the right-hand needle and to the front again, as shown. Purl the next stitch.

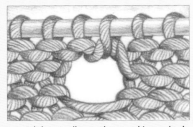

Multiple yarn overs (two or more): Wrap the yarn around the needle, as when working a single yarn over, then continue wrapping the yarn around the needle as many times as indicated. Work the next stitch of the left-hand needle. On the following row, work stitches into the extra yarn overs as described in the pattern. The illustration on the right depicts a finished yarn-over on the purl side.

At the beginning of a knit row: Insert the right-hand needle knitwise into the first stitch on the left-hand needle, keeping the yarn in front of the needle. Bring the yarn over the right-hand needle to the back and knit the first stitch, holding the yarn over with your thumb if necessary.

At the beginning of a purl row: Insert the right-hand needle purlwise into the first stitch on the left-hand needle, keeping the yarn behind the needle. Purl the first stitch.

FIBER FACTS

Yarn content plays a big part in choosing your blocking method. Below are recommendations for some common fibers. If your yarn is a fiber blend, choose the process most compatible with the predominant fiber. When in doubt, test on your gauge swatch.

- ACRYLIC Wet block by spraying; do not press.
- ALPACA Wet block, or dry block with warm steam.
- ANGORA Wet block by spraying.
- CASHMERE Wet block, or dry block with warm or hot steam.
- COTTON Wet block, or dry block with warm or hot steam.
- LINEN Wet block, or dry block with warm or hot steam.
- LUREX Do not block.
- MOHAIR Wet block by spraying.
- WOOL Wet block, or dry block with warm steam.

FRINGE

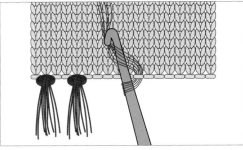

Simple fringe: Cut yarn twice desired length plus extra for knotting. On wrong side, insert hook from front to back through piece and over folded yarn. Pull yarn through. Draw ends through and tighten. Trim yarn.

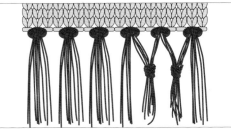

Knotted fringe: After working a simple fringe (it should be longer to allow for extra knotting), take one half of the strands from each fringe and knot them with half the strands from the neighboring fringe.

CARDIGAN CLOUT

(Continued from page 18)

FINISHING

Block pieces to measurements. Sew shoulder seams.

Neckband

With RS facing and smaller needles, pick up and k 122 sts evenly around neck edge. Work in k2, p2 rib as foll: **Next row (WS)** P3, *k2, p2; rep from *, end k2, p3. Cont in rib as established for 1¼"/3cm. Bind off in rib.

Left front band

With RS facing and smaller needles, pick up and k 118 (122, 126) sts evenly along left front edge, including side of neckband. Work in k2, p2 rib for 1¼"/3cm. Bind off in rib. Place markers on band for 6 buttons, the first and last ones ¾"/2cm from each edge and the other 4 spaced evenly between.

Right front band

Work as for left front band, working buttonholes opposite markers after band measures ½"/1.5cm as foll: Bind off 2 sts for each buttonhole. On next row, cast on 2 sts over bound-off sts.

Place markers 10 (10½, 11)"/25.5 (26.5, 28)cm down from shoulders on front and back for armholes. Sew top of sleeves between markers. Sew side and sleeve seams. Sew on buttons.

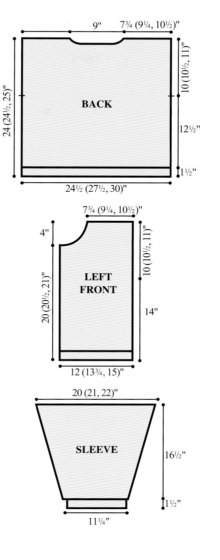

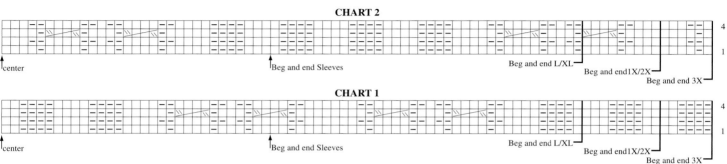

ZIGZAG
(Continued from page 20)

to beg of dpn and bring yarn around from back to k at beg of needle. Rep from * until I-cord measures 33"/84cm. Bind off. Cut 3-12"/30cm pieces of yarn and double as fringe at end of each cord. Sew I-cords to beg of neck edge.

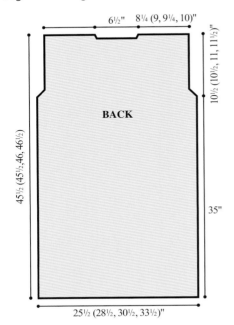

6½"   8¼ (9, 9¼, 10)"

BACK

45½ (45½, 46, 46½)"

10½ (10½, 11, 11½)"

35"

25½ (28½, 30½, 33½)"

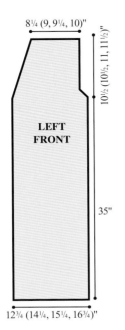

8¼ (9, 9¼, 10)"

LEFT FRONT

10½ (10½, 11, 11½)"

35"

12¾ (14¼, 15¼, 16¾)"

KITCHENER STITCH

1 Insert tapestry needle purlwise (as shown) through first stitch on front needle. Pull yarn through, leaving that stitch on knitting needle.

2 Insert tapestry needle knitwise (as shown) through first stitch on back needle. Pull yarn through, leaving stitch on knitting needle.

3 Insert tapestry needle knitwise through first stitch on front needle, slip stitch off needle and insert tapestry needle purlwise (as shown) through next stitch on front needle. Pull yarn through, leaving this stitch on needle.

4 Insert tapestry needle purlwise through first stitch on back needle. Slip stitch off needle and insert tapestry needle knitwise (as shown) through next stitch on back needle. Pull yarn through, leaving this stitch on needle.

Repeat steps 3 and 4 until all stitches on both front and back needles have been grafted. Fasten off and weave in end.

STRIPE IT UP
(Continued from page 22)

to end. Bind off purlwise working double yo as p1, k1. Sew on button opposite buttonloop.

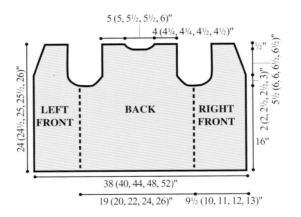

5 (5, 5½, 5½, 6)"

4 (4¼, 4¼, 4½, 4½)"

½"

2 (2, 2½, 2½, 3)"

5½ (6, 6, 6½, 6½)"

24 (24½, 25, 25½, 26)"

LEFT FRONT   **BACK**   **RIGHT FRONT**

16"

38 (40, 44, 48, 52)"

19 (20, 22, 24, 26)"   9½ (10, 11, 12, 13)"

TRUE BLUE

(Continued from page 24)

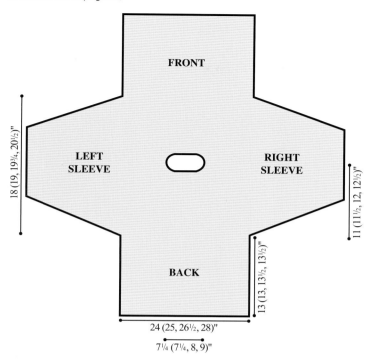

FRONT

LEFT SLEEVE

RIGHT SLEEVE

BACK

18 (19, 19¾, 20½)"

11 (11½, 12, 12½)"

13 (13, 13½, 13½)"

24 (25, 26½, 28)"

7¼ (7¼, 8, 9)"

RED ALERT

(Continued from page 28)

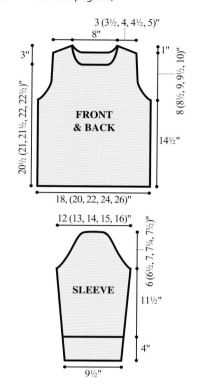

FRONT & BACK

3 (3½, 4, 4½, 5)"

8"

3"

1"

8 (8½, 9, 9½, 10)"

14½"

20½ (21, 21½, 22, 22½)"

18, (20, 22, 24, 26)"

SLEEVE

12 (13, 14, 15, 16)"

6 (6½, 7, 7¼, 7½)"

11½"

4"

9½"

FALL FUZZY

(Continued from page 26)

FINISHING

Block pieces to measurements.

Pocket trims

With smaller needles, pick up and k13 sts across pocket opening, inc 1 st each side of row—15 sts. K 4 rows. Bind off. Sew pocket linings in place. Sew pocket trims to fronts. Sew shoulder seams. Sew sleeves into armholes, sewing the top 2"/5cm (above yarn markers) to 6 bound-off armhole sts. Sew side and sleeve seams.

Collar

With RS facing and smaller needles, pick up and k 56 (56, 60, 60, 60) sts evenly around neck edge, omitting front bands. **Row 1** Sl 1, k to end. Rep this row for garter st until collar measures 2½"/6.5cm. Change to larger needles and cont for 3"/7.5cm more. Bind off. Sew on buttons opposite buttonholes.

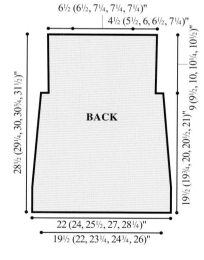

BACK

6½ (6½, 7¼, 7¼, 7¼)"

4½ (5½, 6, 6½, 7¼)"

28½ (29¼, 30, 30¾, 31½)"

9 (9½, 10, 10¼, 10½)"

19½ (19¾, 20, 20½, 21)"

22 (24, 25½, 27, 28¼)"

19½ (22, 23¼, 24¾, 26)"

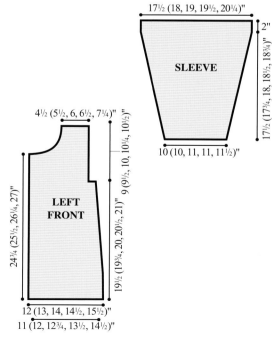

LEFT FRONT

4½ (5½, 6, 6½, 7¼)"

9 (9½, 10, 10¼, 10½)"

24¾ (25½, 26¼, 27)"

19½ (19¾, 20, 20½, 21)"

12 (13, 14, 14½, 15½)"

11 (12, 12¾, 13½, 14½)"

SLEEVE

17½ (18, 19, 19½, 20¼)"

2"

17½ (17¾, 18, 18½, 18¾)"

10 (10, 11, 11, 11½)"

Weather the Cold

SWING KID

(Continued from page 32)

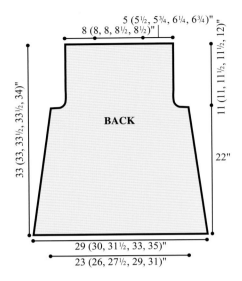

5 (5½, 5¾, 6¼, 6¾)"

8 (8, 8, 8½, 8½)"

33 (33, 33½, 33½, 34)"

BACK

11 (11, 11½, 11½, 12)"

22"

29 (30, 31½, 33, 35)"

23 (26, 27½, 29, 31)"

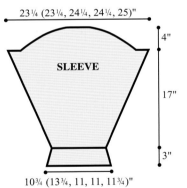

23¼ (23¼, 24¼, 24¼, 25)"

SLEEVE

4"

17"

3"

10¾ (13¾, 11, 11, 11¾)"

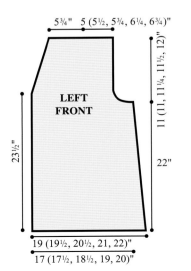

5¾" 5 (5½, 5¾, 6¼, 6¾)"

LEFT
FRONT

11 (11, 11¼, 11½, 12)"

22"

23½"

19 (19½, 20½, 21, 22)"

17 (17½, 18½, 19, 20)"

SWIRL OF GOLD

(Continued from page 34)

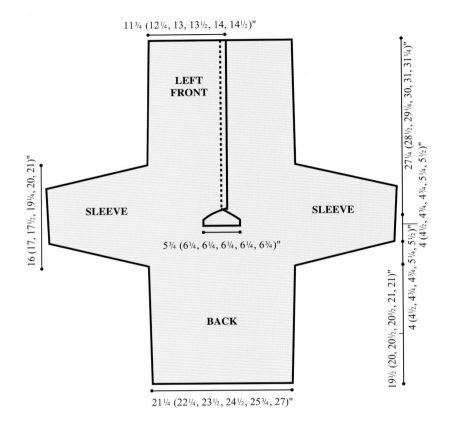

11¾ (12¼, 13, 13½, 14, 14½)"

LEFT
FRONT

SLEEVE

SLEEVE

27¼ (28½, 29¼, 30, 31, 31¼)"

4 (4½, 4¾, 4¾, 5¼, 5½)"

4 (4½, 4¾, 4¾, 5¼, 5½)"

16 (17, 17½, 19¼, 20, 21)"

5¾ (6¼, 6¼, 6¼, 6¼, 6¾)"

BACK

19½ (20, 20½, 20½, 21, 21)"

21¼ (22¼, 23½, 24½, 25¾, 27)"

RED ALL OVER

(Continued from page 36)

and handknitting needles, work 6 rows seed st ending with a WS row. Bind off.

RIGHT FRONT

Work to correspond to left front reversing all shaping.

SLEEVES

With WY cast on 44 (44, 44, 46, 48) sts using the open edge cast-on method and work 6 rows. Break off WY. *Join MC* and inc 1 st each side of every 3rd row once, every 6th row twice, every 12th (10th, 8th, 7th, 6th) row 5 (7, 9, 10, 11) times—60 (64, 68, 72, 76) sts and 84 (84, 87, 87, 90) rows, *17 (17, 17½, 17½, 18½)"/43 (43, 44.5, 44.5, 47)cm.*

CAP SHAPING

Bind off 3 sts at beg of next 2 rows. Dec 1 st each side of next 8 rows. Dec 1 st at beg of next 4 rows. Bind off rem 34 (38, 42, 46, 50) sts. Bind off (machine knit only) as for left back. Remove WY from lower edge and pick up sts with needles. With MC work 6 rows seed st ending with a WS row. Bind off.

FINISHING

Sew center back seam to markers. With right-sides together sew across the tops of the seed st extensions and fold them toward the right back on the WS. Tack the right extension to right back on WS. Sew shoulder seams. Set in sleeves. Sew side and sleeve seams.

Left button band and collar

With handknitting needles cast on 6 sts. Work 21 (21½, 22, 22½, 23)"/53 (55, 56, 57, 58)cm seed st. Inc 1 st at seam edge every other row 10 times, then every 3rd row to 28 sts. Work even until piece fits up left front, up neck shaping and around to the center back seam. Bind off. Sew piece to garment leaving 1"/2.5 cm open at the back neck.

Right buttonhole band and collar

Work to correspond to left button band and collar except place a buttonhole when piece measures 20½ (21, 21½, 22, 22½)"/ 52 (53, 55, 56, 57)cm as foll: work 2 sts pat, bind off 2 sts, work to end. **Next row** Cast on 2 sts over the bound-off sts. Sew piece to garment leaving 1"/2.5cm open at the back neck. Sew two collar pieces tog. Finish sewing collar to back neck.

PATTERN PLAY

(Continued from page 38)

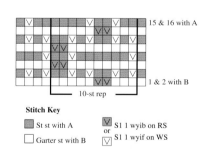

15 & 16 with A

1 & 2 with B

10-st rep

Stitch Key

▨ St st with A	⊻ S1 1 wyib on RS
☐ Garter st with B	or ⊻ S1 1 wyif on WS

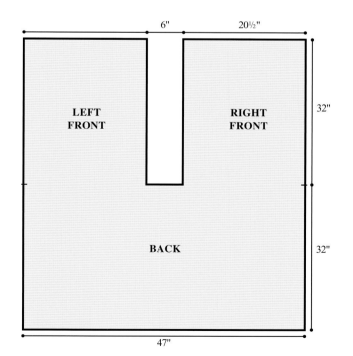

6"   20½"

LEFT FRONT

RIGHT FRONT

32"

BACK

32"

47"

TURNING LEAVES

(Continued from page 40)

sleeve cuff so that seam falls on RS and rem of sleeve seam so that seam is on WS. Leaving 5"/12.5cm free for side slits, sew side seams.

LARGE LEAVES

(make 6 in B and 4 in C.)

With two dpn and B or C, cast on 5 sts. ***Row 1** Knit. Bring yarn around back of needle and back to beg of row just knit. Rep from * (for I-cord) until piece measures 1"/2.5cm from beg.

Beg leaf pat

Row 1 K1, M1, [k1, yo] twice, k1, M1, k1—9 sts. **Row 2 and all even rows, (except 12, 22, and 36)** Purl. **Rows 3, 13 and 23** [K3, yo] twice, k3—11 sts. **Rows 5, 15 and 25** K3, yo, k5, yo, k3—13 sts. **Rows 7 and 17** K3, yo, k7, yo, k3—15 sts. **Rows 9 and 19** K3, yo, k9, yo, k3—17 sts. **Rows 11 and 21** K8, yo, k1, yo, k3, sl last 5 sts to a holder—14 sts. **Rows 12 and 22** P9, sl last 5 sts to a holder—9 sts. **Row 27** Ssk, k1, yo, k2tog, k3, ssk, yo, k1, k2tog—11 sts. **Row 29** Ssk, yo, k2tog, k3, ssk, yo, k2tog—9 sts. **Row 31** Ssk, yo, k2tog, k1, ssk, yo, k2tog—7 sts. **Row 33** Ssk, yo, sl 2 knitwise, k1, pass 2 sl sts one at a time over the k1 st (p2sso), yo, k2tog—5 sts. **Row 35** K1, sl 2 knitwise, k1, p2sso, k1—3 sts. **Row 36** Sl 1 purl-wise, p2tog, psso the p2tog. Fasten off last st.

Side leaves

With RS facing, place 5 sts from upper left holder onto needle. Join yarn. **Row 1** Knit. **Rows 2 and 4** Purl. **Row 3** Ssk, k1, k2tog—3 sts. **Row 5** Sl 2 knitwise, k1, p2sso. Fasten off last st. Rep for lower left holder. With RS facing, place sts from upper right holder onto needle. Join yarn. **Row 1** Ssk, k1, k2tog—3 sts. **Row 2** Purl. **Row 3** Sl 2 knitwise. k1, p2sso. Fasten off last st. Rep for lower right holder.

SMALL LEAVES

(make 5 in A.)

With A, work as for rows 1-22 of leaves. **Row 23** Ssk, k5, k2tog—7 sts. **Row 25** Ssk, k3, k2tog—5 sts. **Row 27** Ssk, k1, k2tog—3 sts. **Row 29** Sl 2 knitwise, k1, p2sso. Fasten off last st. Finish side leaves as for large leaves. Alternating colors and directions of leaves as in photo, sew 3 leaves to right pocket, 2 leaves to left pocket and rem of leaves around shawl collar, beg at 2"/5cm above button/buttonhole. Sew on buttons. Fold cuffs up for 4"/10cm and tack in place.

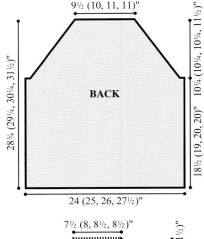

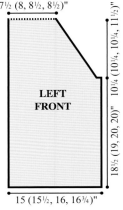

TOGGLES WITH A TWIST

(Continued from page 42)

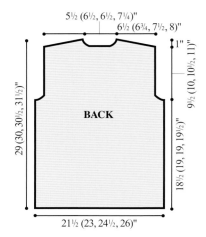

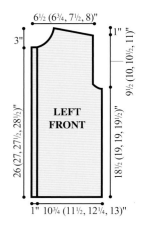

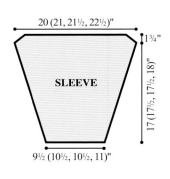

CITY CHIC

(Continued from page 44)

shaping. Work in seed st for 4 rows. Bind off in seed st. Place markers for 7 buttons along left front as foll: the first 4"/10cm above lower edge, the last 2"/5cm below collar, and 5 spaced evenly between. Rep front band for right side, working buttonholes opposite markers as foll: on 2nd row, work seed st to marker, bind off 2 sts. Cast on 2 sts over bound-off sts on next row.

Set in sleeves, sewing last 1½ (1½, 1¾, 1¾)"/4 (4, 4.5, 4.5)cm at top of sleeve to bound-off armhole sts. Sew side and sleeve seams.

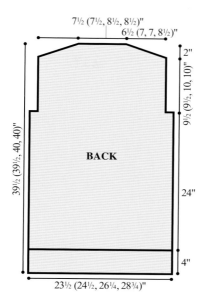

7½ (7½, 8½, 8½)"
6½ (7, 7, 8½)"
2"
9½ (9½, 10, 10)"
39½ (39½, 40, 40)"
BACK
24"
4"
23½ (24½, 26¼, 28¾)"

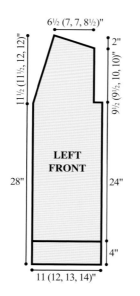

6½ (7, 7, 8½)"
11½ (11½, 12, 12)"
2"
9½ (9½, 10, 10)"
LEFT FRONT
28"
24"
4"
11 (12, 13, 14)"

19 (19, 20, 20)"
SLEEVE
15 (16, 17, 18)"
4"
11 (11, 12, 12)"

SO SIMPLE

(Continued from page 46)

Sew side and sleeve seams. Sew on buttons.

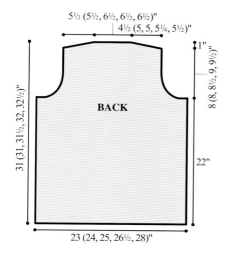

5½ (5½, 6½, 6½, 6½)"
4½ (5, 5, 5¼, 5½)"
1"
8 (8, 8½, 9, 9½)"
31 (31, 31½, 32, 32½)"
BACK
22"
23 (24, 25, 26½, 28)"

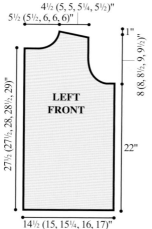

4½ (5, 5, 5¼, 5½)"
5½ (5½, 6, 6, 6)"
1"
8 (8, 8½, 9, 9½)"
27½ (27½, 28, 28½, 29)"
LEFT FRONT
22"
14½ (15, 15¼, 16, 17)"

16¾ (16¾, 17½, 18½, 19¼)"
6 (6, 6½, 7, 7½)"
16½ (16½, 16½, 17, 17)"
SLEEVE
10½ (10½, 11¼, 11¼, 12)"

(Continued from page 48)

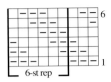

6

1

6-st rep

Stitch Key

☐ K on RS, p on WS

⊟ P on RS, k on WS

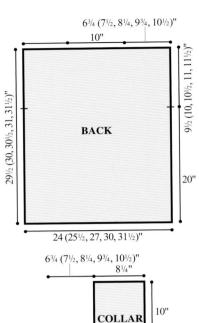

6¾ (7½, 8¼, 9¾, 10½)"
10"

BACK

29½ (30, 30½, 31, 31½)"

9½ (10, 10½, 11, 11½)"

20"

24 (25½, 27, 30, 31½)"

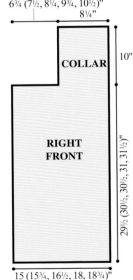

6¾ (7½, 8¼, 9¾, 10½)"
8¼"

COLLAR

10"

RIGHT FRONT

29½ (30½, 30½, 31, 31½)"

15 (15¾, 16½, 18, 18¾)"

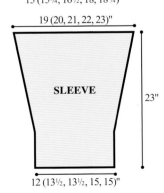

19 (20, 21, 22, 23)"

SLEEVE

23"

12 (13½, 13½, 15, 15)"

WARM FRONT

(Continued from page 50)

Pocket trims

With smaller needles, pick up and k13 sts across pocket opening, inc 1 st each side of row—15 sts. K 4 rows. Bind off. Sew pocket linings in place. Sew pocket trims to fronts. Sew shoulder seams. Sew sleeves into armholes, sewing the top 2"/5cm (above yarn markers) to 6 bound-off armhole sts. Sew side and sleeve seams.

Collar

With RS facing and smaller needles, pick up and k 56 (56, 60, 60, 60) sts evenly around neck edge, omitting front bands. **Row 1** Sl 1, k to end. Rep this row for garter st until collar measures 2½"/6.5cm. Change to larger needles and cont for 3"/7.5cm more. Bind off. Sew on buttons opposite buttonholes.

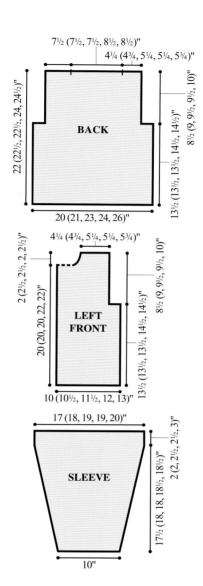

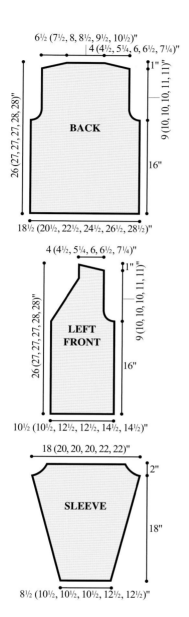

Sophisticated Styles

A SWEATER FOR ALL SEASONS

(Continued from page 56)

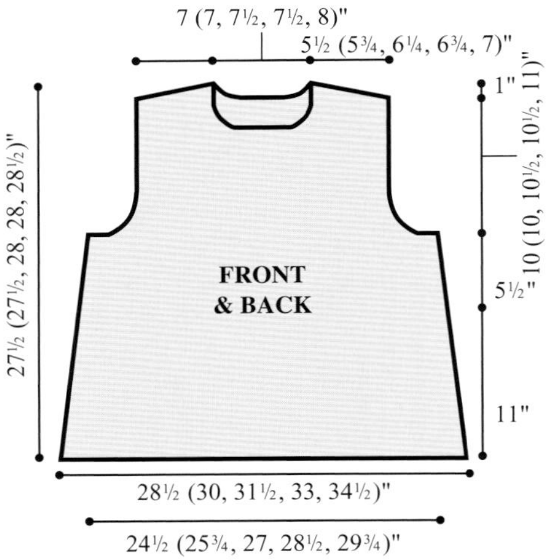
7 (7, 7½, 7½, 8)"
5½ (5¾, 6¼, 6¾, 7)"
1"
10 (10, 10½, 10½, 11)"
5½"
11"
27½ (27½, 28, 28, 28½)"
FRONT & BACK
28½ (30, 31½, 33, 34½)"
24½ (25¾, 27, 28½, 29¾)"

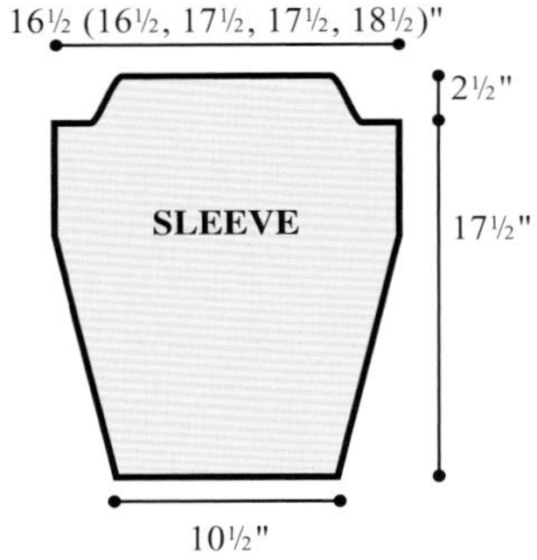
16½ (16½, 17½, 17½, 18½)"
2½"
17½"
SLEEVE
10½"

BRAVO FOR BOBBLES

(Continued from page 58)

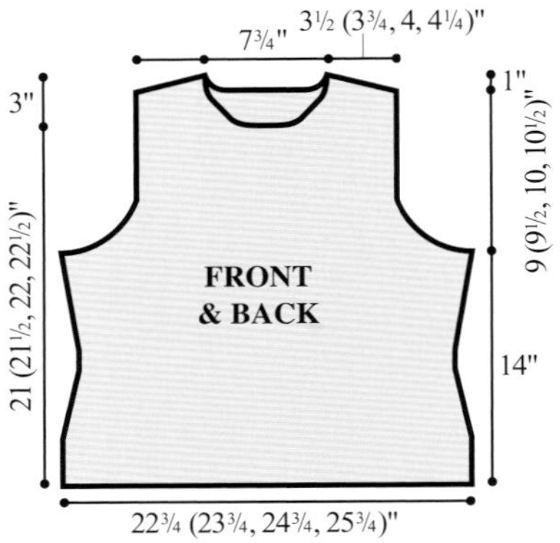
7¾"
3½ (3¾, 4, 4¼)"
3"
1"
9 (9½, 10, 10½)"
14"
21 (21½, 22, 22½)"
FRONT & BACK
22¾ (23¾, 24¾, 25¾)"

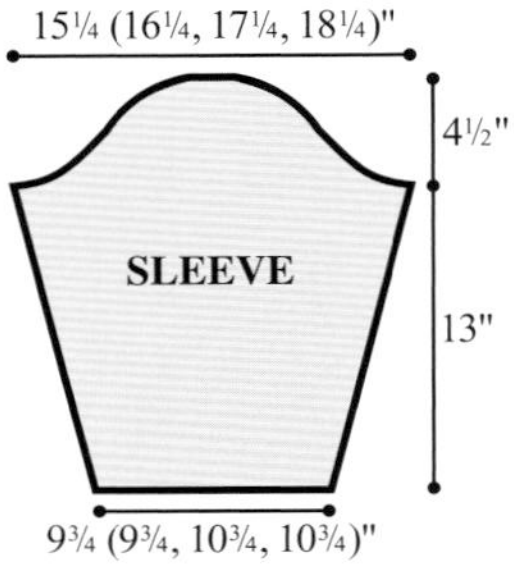
15¼ (16¼, 17¼, 18¼)"
4½"
SLEEVE
13"
9¾ (9¾, 10¾, 10¾)"

WHITE HEAT

(Continued from page 60)

FINISHING

Block pieces to measurements. With smaller needles, pick up and k 7 sts along one side of front neck slit. Bind off knitwise. Work other side of slit in same way. Sew shoulder seams. With circular needle, pick up and k 47 (47, 50, 50) sts evenly around neck edge. Bind off knitwise. Sew sleeves into armholes. Sew side and sleeve seams.

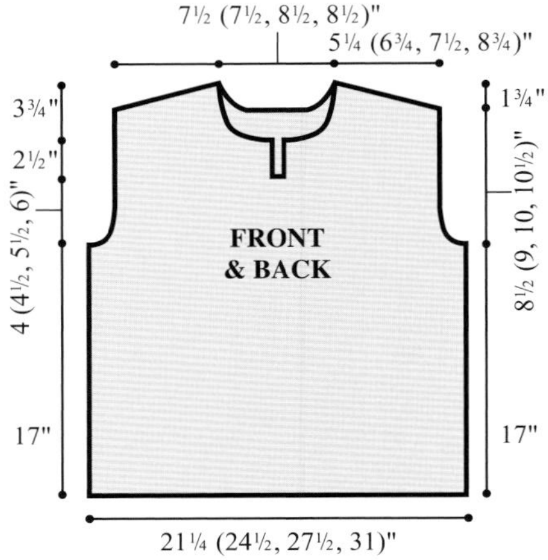
7½ (7½, 8½, 8½)"
5¼ (6¾, 7½, 8¾)"
3¾"
2½"
4 (4½, 5½, 6)"
1¾"
8½ (9, 10, 10½)"
FRONT & BACK
17"
17"
21¼ (24½, 27½, 31)"

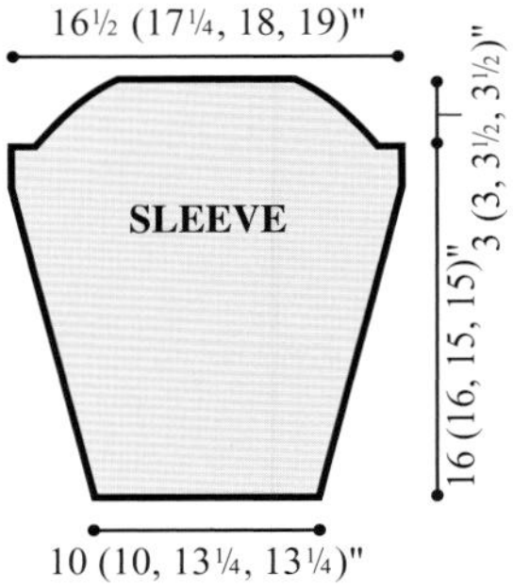
16½ (17¼, 18, 19)"
3 (3, 3½, 3½)"
16 (16, 15, 15)"
SLEEVE
10 (10, 13¼, 13¼)"

EYE-CATCHING EYELET

(Continued from page 62)

Neckband

With RS facing and circular needles, pick up and k 34 (36, 36, 38, 38) sts along back neck, 24 (25, 25, 28, 28) sts along left front neck, pm, 2 sts at center front neck, pm, 24 (25, 25, 28, 28) sts along left front neck—84 (88, 88, 96, 96) sts. Join and work as foll: **Dec rnd** Beg with p2 (p1, p1, p2) work in k2, p2 rib to 2 sts before center marked sts, SKP, sl marker, k2, sl marker, k2tog, beg with k2 rib to end of rnd. Rib 1 rnd even. Rep last 2 rnds until band measures 1½"/4cm. Bind off in rib.

Place markers 9½ (10, 10½, 11, 11½)"/24 (25.5, 26.5, 28, 29)cm down from shoulder seams on front and back for armholes. Sew top of sleeves between markers. Sew side and sleeve seams.

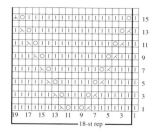

Stitch Key

☐ P on WS ⟍ SKP

│ K on RS ⟑ Dec 2

⟍ K2tog ○ Yo

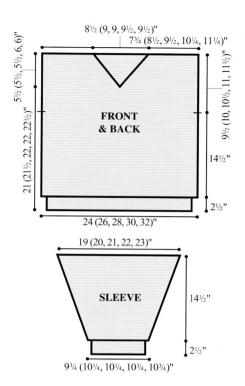

ENCHANTED EVENING

(Continued from page 64)

Stitch Key

● = Picot st

— = Joining st

URBAN OUTFITTER

(Continued from page 66)

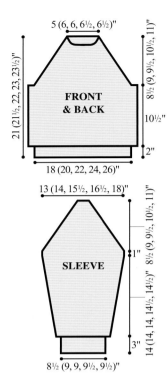

5 (6, 6, 6½, 6½)"

21 (21½, 22, 23, 23½)"

8½ (9, 9½, 10½, 11)"

FRONT & BACK

10½"

2"

18 (20, 22, 24, 26)"

13 (14, 15½, 16½, 18)"

SLEEVE

8½ (9, 9½, 10½, 11)"

1"

8½ (9, 9½, 10½, 11)"

14 (14, 14, 14½, 14½)"

3"

8½ (9, 9, 9½, 9½)"

FAUX FABULOUS

(Continued from page 68)

RIGHT FRONT

Work as for left front, reversing placement of front band and all shaping.

SLEEVES

With 1 strand A and B held tog, cast on 26 (26, 26, 28, 28) sts. **Row 1 (WS)** Knit. **Row 2 (RS)** With 2 strands C, knit. Change back to 1 strand A and B held tog and beg with a purl (WS) row, work in St st until piece measures 6½ (6½, 6, 6, 5½)"/16 (16, 15, 15, 14)cm from beg. **Inc row** K1, M1, k to last st, M1, k1. Rep inc row every 4th row 7 (8, 9, 9, 10) times more—42 (44, 46, 48, 50) sts. Work even until piece measures 17½ (17½, 17¾, 18, 18½)"/44 (44, 45, 46, 47)cm from beg.

Cap shaping

Bind off 2 sts at beg of next 2 rows. Work dec row as on back armhole on next row then every other row 5 times more. Bind off rem 26 (28, 30, 32, 34) sts.

FINISHING

Block pieces to measurements.

Pocket trims

Locating 9 sts from center front at 6"/15cm from lower edge, with 1 strand A and B held tog, pick up and k 11 (11, 11, 12, 12) sts straight across as in photo, then with 2 strands C, k1 row, p1 row, then with 1 strand A and B held tog, k1 row and bind off purlwise. Make other pocket trim in same way. Sew sides of trims to fronts. Sew shoulder seams including front band seams.

Back neck trim

With 2 strands C, pick up and k sts around inside of back neck seed st edge to correspond to front band edge in C. Bind off knitwise. Set in sleeves. Sew side and sleeve seams.

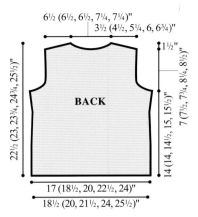

6½ (6½, 6½, 7¼, 7¼)"

3½ (4½, 5¼, 6, 6¾)"

1½"

BACK

22½ (23, 23¾, 24¾, 25½)"

7 (7½, 7¾, 8¼, 8½)"

14 (14, 14½, 15, 15½)"

17 (18½, 20, 22½, 24)"

18½ (20, 21½, 24, 25½)"

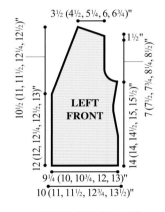

3½ (4½, 5¼, 6, 6¾)"

1½"

LEFT FRONT

10½ (11, 11½, 12¼, 12½)"

12 (12, 12¼, 12½, 13)"

7 (7½, 7¾, 8¼, 8½)"

14 (14, 14½, 15, 15½)"

9¼ (10, 10¾, 12, 13)"

10 (11, 11½, 12¾, 13½)"

17 (17½, 18½, 19¼, 20)"

3¼"

SLEEVE

17½ (17½, 17¾, 18, 18½)"

10½ (10½, 10½, 11¼, 11¼)"

PULLOVER POLISH

(Continued from page 70)

Beg front neck

Next row (RS) With MC, knit. **Next row (WS)** Bind off 3 sts, p to end. Cont to shape neck binding off at beg of p rows 2 sts 3 times more—85 sts. **Next (short) row (RS)** With CC, k55, w&t. With CC, p to end. With MC, work in St st for 6 rows dec 1 st at neck edge every WS row 3 times—82 sts. With MC, work 2 rows in St st. **Next (short) row (RS)** With CC, k25, w&t. With CC, p to end. With MC, work 2 rows iin St st. **Next row (RS)** With MC, knit to last st, M1, k1.Purl 1 row. Rep last 2 rows twice more—85sts. **Next (short) row (RS)** With CC, k 65, w&t. With CC, purl to end. **Next row (RS)** With MC, knit to end casting on 2 sts at end of row. Purl 1 row. rep last 2 rows twice more—91 sts. **Next row (RS)** K to end, casting on 3 sts at end of row—94 sts. Purl 1 row. **Next (short) row (RS)** With CC, k38, w&t, with CC, p to end. This is end of neck shaping. Then beg at 2nd + on back, complete as for back.

SLEEVES

Beg at side seam with MC, cast on 8 sts. P1 row. Cont in St st with MC and cast on at beg of RS rows, 8 sts twice—24sts. At beg of next RS row, cast on 40 sts—64 sts. Cont in St st with MC and cast on at beg of RS rows, 2 sts 3 times—70 sts. **Next (short) row (RS)** With MC, knit, castiing on 2 sts at end of row. With MC, purl 1 row*. Rep between *'s 3 times more—78sts. **Next (short) row (RS)** With CC, k29, w&t. With CC, p to end. Rep between *'s 3 times more—84 sts. With MC, work 2 rows even in St st. **Next (short) row (RS)** With CC, k45, w&t. With CC, p to end. With MC, work 8 rows even in St st. This marks the center of the sleeve. **Next (short) row (RS)** With CC, k23, w&t. With CC, p to end. With MC, work 8 rows even in St st. **Next (short) row (RS)** With CC, k52, w&t. With CC, p to end. With MC, work 2 rows even in St st. **. Rep between **'s twice more—78 sts. **Next (short) row (RS)** With CC, k38, w&t. With CC, p to end. Rep between **'s 4 times more—70 sts. **Next (short) row (RS)** With CC, k15, w&t. With CC, p to end. Rep between **'s 3 times more—64 sts. **Next row (RS)** Bind off 40 sts, k to end—24 sts. P1 row. **Next row (RS)** Bind off 8 sts, k to end—8 sts. P 1 row. Bind off rem 8 sts.

FINISHING

Block pieces to measurements. Sew shoulder seams. Set in sleeves. Sew side and sleeve seams.

Neck trim

With circular needle and CC, pick up and k 60 sts evenly around neck edge. Join and pl rnd. Bind off purlwise.

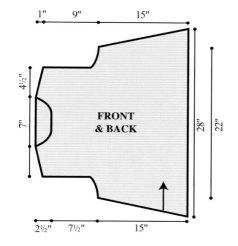

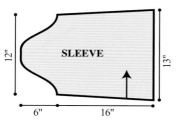

FRINGED BENEFITS

(Continued from page 72)

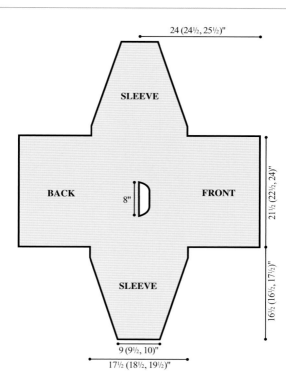

AUTUMN HARVEST

(Continued from page 74)

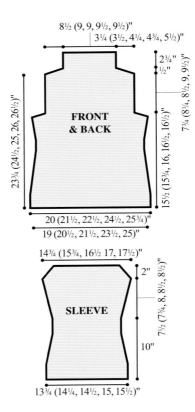

8½ (9, 9, 9½, 9½)"

3¼ (3½, 4¼, 4¾, 5½)"

2¾"

½"

FRONT & BACK

23¾ (24½, 25, 26, 26½)"

7¾ (8¼, 8½, 9, 9½)"

15½ (15¾, 16, 16½, 16½)"

20 (21½, 22½, 24½, 25¾)"

19 (20½, 21½, 23½, 25)"

14¾ (15¾, 16½ 17, 17½)"

2"

SLEEVE

7½ (7¾, 8, 8½)"

10"

13¾ (14¼, 14½, 15, 15½)"

BLUE CROSS

(Continued from page 76)

FRONT

Work as for back until armhole measures 6½ (7, 7½)"/16.5 (18, 19)cm.

Neck shaping

Next row (RS) Work 28 (29, 30) sts, join a 2nd ball of yarn and bind off center 8 (10, 12) sts, work to end. Work both sides at once for 1 row more. **Next row (RS)** Work to last 4 sts of first side, k3tog, p1; on 2nd side, p1, SK2P, work to end. Work 1 row even. Rep last 2 rows twice more. **Next row (RS)** Work to last 3 sts of first side, k2tog, p1; on 2nd side, p1, SKP, work to end. Work 1 row even. Rep last 2 rows once more, AT SAME TIME, shape shoulders when same length as back.

SLEEVES

Cast on 32 (36, 36) sts. **Row 1 (RS)** P2 (0, 0), work k2, p2 rib over 12 (16, 16) sts, FC, p2, work k2, p2 rib over 12 (14, 14) sts. Cont to work in this way for 2½"/6.5cm, end with a WS row. **Next row (RS)** P14 (16, 16), FC, p14 (16, 16). Cont in pats as established inc 1 st each side (working inc sts into rev St st) every 6th row 8 times every 4th row 4 (4, 6) times—56 (60, 64) sts. Work even until piece measures 17½ (18, 18)"/44.5 (45.5, 45.5)cm from beg.

Cap shaping

Bind off 4 sts at beg of next 2 rows, 2 sts at beg of next 2 rows. Dec 1 st each side every other row 12 times. Bind off rem 20 (24, 28) sts. Make a 2nd sleeve in same way with BC instead of FC.

FINISHING

Block pieces to measurements. Sew right shoulder seam.

Turtleneck

Pick up and k 86 (90, 94) sts evenly around neck edge. Work in k2, p2 rib for 7"/18cm. Bind off loosely in rib. Sew left shoulder and turtle-neck seam, sewing top half of turtleneck from opposite side for foldback of collar. Set in sleeves. Sew side and sleeve seams.

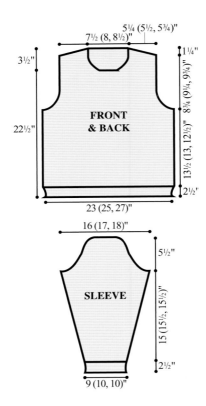

5¼ (5½, 5¾)"

7½ (8, 8½)"

1¼"

3½"

FRONT & BACK

22½"

8¾ (9¼, 9¾)"

13½ (13, 12½)"

2½"

23 (25, 27)"

16 (17, 18)"

5½"

SLEEVE

15 (15½, 15½)"

2½"

9 (10, 10)"

CABLE VISION

(Continued from page 78)

SLEEVES

With smaller needles, cast on 49 (51, 53, 55) sts. Work twisted rib for 2½"/6.5cm, inc 9 (7, 7, 9) sts evenly across last (WS) row—58 (58, 60, 64) sts. Change to larger needles.

Beg chart

Next row (RS) K14 (14, 15, 17), work row 1 of Cable chart over 30 sts, k14 (14, 15, 17). Cont in pat as established, AT SAME TIME, inc 1 st each side (working inc sts into St st) every 6th (6th, 4th, 4th) row 7 (16, 1, 1) times, every 8th (0, 6th, 6th) row 6 (0, 16, 16) times—84 (90, 94, 98) sts. Work even until piece measures 17 (18, 18½, 18½)"/43 (46, 47, 47)cm from beg, end with a WS row. Place a marker at each side of row.

Cap shaping

Work even for 1½ (1½, 2, 2¼)"/4 (4.5, 5, 5.5)cm, end with a WS row. Dec 1 st each side on next row, then every other row 3 (3, 3, 4) times more. Bind off rem 76 (82, 86, 88) sts.

FINISHING

Block pieces. Sew shoulder seams.

Neckband

With RS facing and circular needle, sl 14 (16, 18, 19) sts of right front holder to needle, join 2nd ball of yarn and pick up and k 61 (65, 69, 75) sts evenly around neck edge, work twisted rib across 14 (16, 18, 19) sts of left front holder—89 (97, 105, 113) sts. Cont in rib pat until neckband measures 1"/2.5cm. Bind off in pat. Set in sleeves, matching markers to underarm seam. Sew side and sleeve seams. Sew in zipper.

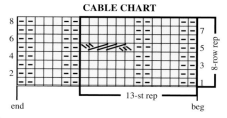

CABLE CHART

Stitch Key

☐ k on RS, p on WS

⊟ p on RS, k on WS

6-st cable

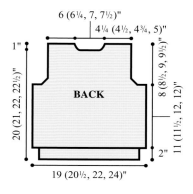

BACK

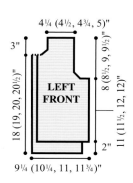

LEFT FRONT

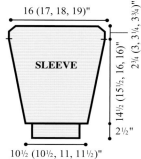

SLEEVE

SHEER DELIGHT

(Continued from page 80)

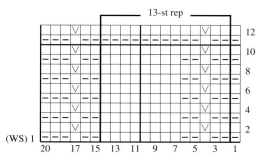

Stitch Key

☐ K on RS, p on WS

⊟ P on RS, k on WS

⋁ K1 in row below (K1-b)

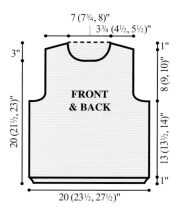

FRONT & BACK

SLEEVE

Soak Up the Sun

IN BLOOM

(Continued from page 84)

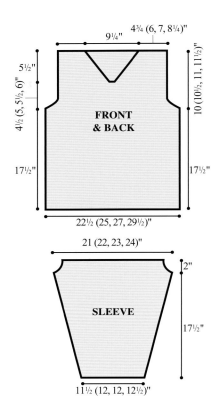

FRONT & BACK

9¼"
4¾ (6, 7, 8¼)"
5½"
4½ (5, 5½, 6)"
10 (10½, 11, 11½)"
17½"
17½"
22½ (25, 27, 29½)"

SLEEVE

21 (22, 23, 24)"
2"
17½"
11½ (12, 12, 12½)"

Stitch Key

- ☐ purl all WS rows
- Ⅰ Knit
- ⧄ K2tog
- ⧅ SKP
- ⊼ dec2
- ○ Yo

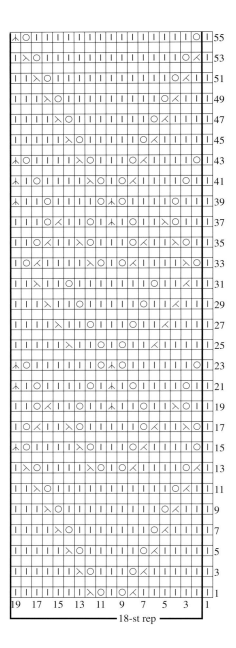

19 17 15 13 11 9 7 5 3 1

55 53 51 49 47 45 43 41 39 37 35 33 31 29 27 25 23 21 19 17 15 13 11 9 7 5 3 1

— 18-st rep —

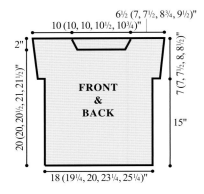

FRONT & BACK

6½ (7, 7½, 8¾, 9½)"
10 (10, 10, 10½, 10¾)"
2"
20 (20, 20½, 21, 21½)"
7 (7, 7½, 8, 8½)"
15"
18 (19¼, 20, 23¼, 25¼)"

THINK PINK

(Continued from page 90)

markers for six buttons evenly spaced, having the first one at $^1/_2$"/1.25cm from lower edge, the last one at beg of neck shaping and the others evenly spaced between. Work right front band to correspond, working yo, p2tog buttonholes to correspond to markers. Sew shoulder seams. Sew bands to neck edge.

COLLAR

With smaller needles and 3 strands of yarn, pick up and k 50 (50, 50, 54) sts evenly around neck edges, beg and end at ends of front band. Work in k2, p2 rib for $2^1/_2$"/6.5cm. Bind off in rib. Sew six bound-off sts of each band to corresponding $1^1/_2$"/4cm of collar sides. Sew sleeves into armholes. Sew side and sleeve seams.

Picot edge

With crochet hook and 1 strand of yarn, work edge around sleeve cuffs as foll: Join in seam, 1 sc in joining, *ch 4 and skip 3 sts, sl st in next st, ch 4 and sl st in same st (for picot); rep from * around. Join and fasten off. Work edge along lower edge of ribbing in same way. Sew on buttons.

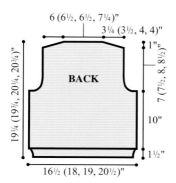

6 (6½, 6½, 7¼)"
3¼ (3½, 4, 4)"
1"
BACK
19¼ (19¾, 20¼, 20¾)"
7 (7½, 8, 8½)"
10"
1½"
16½ (18, 19, 20½)"

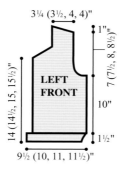

3¼ (3½, 4, 4)"
1"
7 (7½, 8, 8½)"
LEFT FRONT
10"
1½"
14 (14½, 15, 15½)"
9½ (10, 11, 11½)"

13 (14, 14½, 15¼)"
3¼ (3¾, 4¼, 4¾)"
SLEEVE
15"
2"
7¼ (7¼, 7¼, 8¾)"

MESH MARVEL

(Continued from page 92)

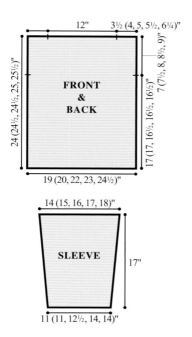

12"
3½ (4, 5, 5½, 6¼)"
7 (7½, 8, 8½, 9)"
FRONT & BACK
24 (24½, 24½, 25, 25½)"
17 (17, 16½, 16½, 16½)"
19 (20, 22, 23, 24½)"

14 (15, 16, 17, 18)"
SLEEVE
17"
11 (11, 12½, 14, 14)"

FIESTAWEAR

(Continued from page 96)

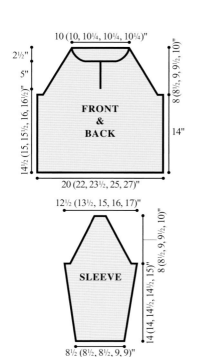

10 (10, 10¼, 10¼, 10¼)"
2½"
5"
8 (8½, 9, 9½, 10)"
14½ (15, 15½, 16, 16½)"
FRONT & BACK
14"
20 (22, 23½, 25, 27)"

12½ (13½, 15, 16, 17)"
8 (8½, 9, 9½, 10)"
SLEEVE
14 (14, 14½, 14½, 15)"
8½ (8½, 8½, 9, 9)"

His 'n Hers

THE TWO OF US

(Continued from page 100)

row with F, work 7 rows in rib with F. P 1 row with A, then cont with stripe pat beg at *, AT SAME TIME, inc 1 st each side every 4th row 9 (10, 12, 14) times—50 (52, 56, 60) sts. Work even until piece measures 17"/43cm, end with same row as back armhole.

Cap shaping

Bind off 3 (3, 3, 4) sts at beg of next 2 rows, 2 sts at beg of next 2 rows, dec 1 st each side of next row then every other row 3 (4, 5, 5) times more. Bind off 3 (3, 4, 4) sts at beg of next 4 rows. Bind off rem 20 (20, 18, 20) sts.

FINISHING

Block pieces to measurements. Sew one shoulder seam.

Turtleneck

With smaller needles and D, pick up and k 70 sts evenly around neck edge, including sts from holders. Work in k3, p2 rib (cont rib as established with sts on holders) for 3"/7.5cm. Then change to p3, k2 rib (for collar foldback) and cont in rib for 3"/7.5cm more. With C, k next row on RS then bind off in rib with C. Sew turtleneck seam, sewing top half so that seam folds back to WS and sew shoulder seam. Sew sleeves into armholes. Sew side and sleeve seams.

WOMEN'S PULLOVER

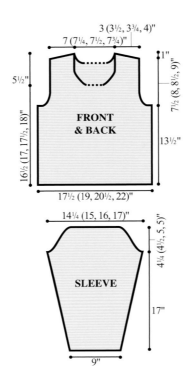

MEN'S VEST

FINISHED MEASUREMENTS

■ Chest 40 (42, 44, 46, 48)"/101.5 (106.5, 111.5, 117, 122)cm

■ Length 25 (25½, 25½, 26, 26½)"/63.5 (65, 65, 66, 67.5)cm

GAUGE

11 sts and 14 rows to 4"/10cm over St st using larger needles.
TAKE TIME TO CHECK YOUR GAUGE.

BACK

With smaller needles and A, cast on 50 (54, 58, 62, 62) sts. Work in k2, p2 rib for 1 row. Change to MC and p next WS row. **Next row** With MC, work in k2, p2 rib. With B, p 1 row. **Next row** With B, work in k2, p2 rib. With MC, p 1 row. With MC, work 2 rows in k2, p2 rib. Change to larger needles, and k next row, inc 5 (4, 3, 2, 4) sts evenly spaced—55 (58, 61, 64, 66) sts. Work even in St st until piece measures 14½"/37cm from beg.

Armhole shaping

Bind off 2 (3, 3, 3, 3) sts at beg of next 2 rows, 2 sts at beg of next 2 rows. Dec 1 st each side of next row, then every other row 1 (1, 2, 3, 3) times more—43 (44, 45, 46, 48) sts. Work even until armhole measures 9½ (10, 10, 10½, 11)"/24 (25.5, 25.5, 26.5, 28)cm.

Neck and shoulder shaping

Bind off 5 (5, 5, 5, 6) sts at beg of next 2 rows, 6 sts at beg of next 2 rows, AT SAME TIME, bind off center 11 (12, 13, 14, 14) sts for neck and working both sides at once, bind off 5 sts from each neck edge once.

FRONT

Work as for back until armhole measures 2 (2½, 2½, 3, 3½)"/5 (6.5, 6.5, 7.5, 9)cm.

V-neck shaping

Next row (RS) Work to center 1 (2, 1, 2, 2) sts, join 2nd ball of yarn and bind off these sts, work to end. Working both sides at once, dec 1 st at each neck edge every other row 10 (10, 11, 11, 11) times—11 (11, 11, 11, 12) sts rem each side. When same length as back, shape shoulders as for back.

FINISHING

Block pieces to measurements. Sew shoulder seams.

Neckband

With RS facing, circular needle and MC, pick up and k 94 (98, 98, 102, 102) sts evenly around neck edge. Do not join, but work back and forth in rows. Work in k2, p2 rib for 3 rows. K 1 row with B, work 1 row in rib with B. K 1 row with MC, work 1 row in rib with MC. K 1 row

with A, then bind off in k2, p2 rib with A. Overlap front neckband (right over left) at center front and sew in place.

Armhole bands

With smaller needles and MC, pick up and k 70 (74, 74, 78, 82) sts evenly around armhole edge. Work in rib as on neckband. Sew side and armhole band seams.

MEN'S VEST

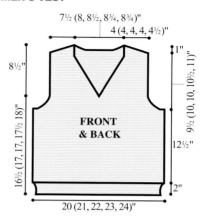

MAN'S BEST FRIEND

(Continued from page 102)

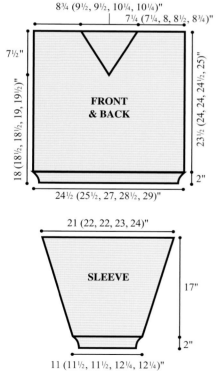

THE NATURAL

(Continued from page 104)

Stitch Key
| I | K on RS, p on WS |
| □ | P on RS, k on WS |

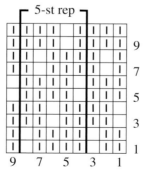

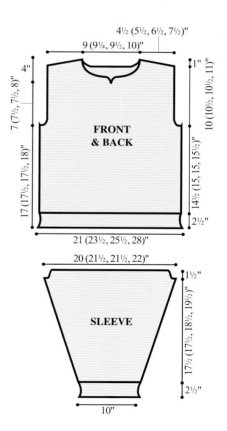

SPORTY STRIPES

(Continued from page 106)

GAUGE

12 sts and 18 rows to 4"/10cm over St st using 2 strands of yarn held tog and larger needles. TAKE TIME TO CHECK YOUR GAUGE.

Note

Work with two strands of yarn held tog throughout.

STRIPE PATTERN

Working with 2 strands of yarn, work *4 rows with B and C, 4 rows with C and D, 2 rows with D and E, 2 rows with E and F, 2 rows with D and E, 4 rows with C and D, 4 rows with B and C, 6 rows with A and B; rep from * (28 rows) for stripe pat.

BACK

With smaller needles and 1 strand A and B, cast on 60 (66, 72, 78, 84) sts.
Row 1 (RS) *P1, k1 tbl; rep from * to end.
Row 2 *P1 tbl, k1; rep from * to end. Rep these 2 rows for twisted rib for 2½"/6.5cm. Change to larger needles, and cont in St st and stripe pat until piece measures 23½ (23½, 24½, 24½, 25½)"/59.5 (59.5, 62, 62, 65)cm from beg.

Neck and shoulder shaping

Next row (RS) Work 20 (23, 25, 28, 30) sts, join another 2 strands of yarn and bind off center 20 (20, 22, 22, 24) sts, work to end. Working both sides at once, bind off 1 st from each neck edge twice. Bind off rem 18 (21, 23, 26, 28) sts each side for shoulders.

FRONT

Work as for back until piece measures 22½ (22½, 23½, 23½, 24½)"/57 (57, 59.5, 59.5, 62)cm from beg.

Neck shaping

Next row (RS) Work 23 (26, 28, 31, 33) sts, join another 2 strands of yarn and bind off center 14 (14, 16, 16, 18) sts, work to end. Working both sides at once, bind off 2 sts from each neck edge twice, 1 st once—18 (21, 23, 26, 28) sts rem each side for shoulders. When same length as back, bind off rem sts each side for shoulders.

SLEEVES

With smaller needles and 1 strand each A and B, cast on 30 (30, 32, 32, 34) sts. Work in k1, p1 twisted rib for 2½"/6.5cm. Change to larger needles and cont in St st and stripe pat, inc 1 st each side every 4th row 8 (8, 9, 9, 9) times, every 6th row 7 times—60 (60, 64, 64, 66) sts. Work even until piece measures 22½"/57cm from beg. Bind off.

FINISHING

Block pieces to measurements. Sew shoulder seams.

Neckband

With circular needle and 1 strand each A and B, pick up and k 66 (66, 68, 68, 68) sts evenly around neck edge. Join.
Rnd 1 *K1 tbl, p1; rep from * around. Rep rnd 1 for twisted rib for 1¼"/3cm. Bind off. Place markers at 10 (10, 10¾, 10¾, 11)"/25.5 (25.5, 27, 27, 28)cm down from shoulders. Sew sleeves to armholes between markers. Sew side and sleeve seams.

MEN'S VERSION

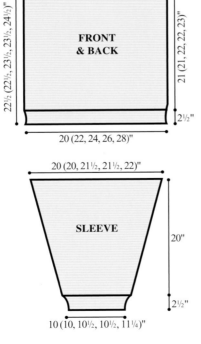

WOMEN'S VERSION

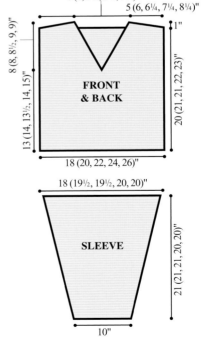

His 'n Hers

23½ (24, 24½, 25, 25½)"/59.5 (61, 62, 63.5, 65)cm from beg.

Neck shaping

Next row (RS) K16 (18, 20, 21, 23) sts, place center 14 (14, 14, 16, 16) sts on a holder for neck, join 2nd ball of yarns and work to end. Working both sides at once, dec 1 st from each neck edge every other row twice. When same length as back, shape shoulders as for back.

SLEEVES

With 1 strand each A, B and C, cast on 18 (22, 22, 22, 22) sts. Work in k2, p2 rib for 3"/7.5cm. Then work in St st, inc 1 st each side every other row 4 (2, 4, 6, 6) times, every 4th row 9 (10, 9, 8, 8) times—44 (46, 48, 50, 50) sts. Work even until piece measures 18"/45.5cm from beg. Bind off.

FINISHING

Block pieces to measurements. Sew shoulder seams. Place markers at 9½ (10½, 10½, 11, 11)"/24 (27, 27, 28, 28)cm down from shoulders. Sew sleeves to armholes between markers. Sew side and sleeve seams.

Neckband

With circular needle and 1 strand each A, B and C, pick up and k 52 (52, 52, 56, 56) sts evenly around neck edge, including sts from holders. Join and work in rnds of St st for 2½"/6.5cm. Bind off loosely.

WOMEN'S SWEATER

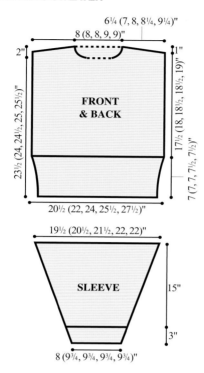

6¼ (7, 8, 8¼, 9¼)"
8 (8, 8, 9, 9)"
2"
1"
FRONT & BACK
23½ (24, 24½, 25, 25½)"
17½ (18, 18½, 18½, 19)"
7 (7, 7½, 7½)"
20½ (22, 24, 25½, 27½)"

19½ (20½, 21½, 22, 22)"
SLEEVE
15"
3"
8 (9¾, 9¾, 9¾, 9¾)"

MEN'S CARDIGAN

FINISHED MEASUREMENTS

▪ Chest 44½ (48, 51, 55, 59)"/113 (122, 129.5, 139.5, 150)cm

▪ Length 27 (27½, 28, 28½, 29)"/68.5 (70, 71, 72.5, 73.5)cm

▪ Upper arm 21½ (22, 22, 23, 23)"/55 (56, 56, 58, 58)cm

GAUGE

9 sts and 13 rows to 4"/10cm over St st using 2 strands A and 1 strand B held tog and size 13 (9mm) needles.
TAKE TIME TO CHECK YOUR GAUGE.

BACK

With 2 strands A and 1 of B held tog, cast on 50 (54, 58, 62, 66) sts. **Row 1 (RS)** K2, *p2, k2; rep from * to end. **Row 2** K the knit sts and p the purl sts. Cont in k2, p2 rib until piece measures 5 (5½, 6, 6, 6½)"/12.5 (14, 15, 15, 16.5)cm from beg. Then work in St st until piece measures 26 (26½, 27, 27½, 28)"/66 (67, 68.5, 70, 71)cm from beg.

Shoulder shaping

Bind off 8 (9, 9, 10, 11) sts at beg of next 2 rows, 8 (9, 10, 11, 12) sts at beg of next 2 rows. Place rem 18 (18, 20, 20, 20) sts on a holder for back neck.

POCKET LINING

(make 2)

With 2 strands A and 1 strand B, cast on 12 sts. Work in St st for 4"/10cm. Place sts on a holder.

RIGHT FRONT

With 2 strands A and 1 strand B, cast on 23 (25, 27, 29, 31) sts. **Row 1 (RS)** P1, *k2, p2; rep from *, end k2 (0, 2, 0, 2). **Row 2** K the knit sts and p the purl sts. Cont in k2, p2 rib until same length as back rib.

POCKET OPENING

Next row (RS) K5 (6, 7, 8, 9), bind off next 12 sts, work to end. On next row, replace bound-off sts with pocket lining sts and cont in St st until piece measures 19¼ (19¾, 20¼, 20¾, 21¼)"/49 (50, 51.5, 52.5, 54)cm from beg, end with a WS row.

Neck shaping

Dec row (RS) K1, ssk, k to end. Rep dec row every other row 2 (2, 4, 4, 4) times more, then every 4th row 4 (4, 3, 3, 3) times—16 (18, 19, 21, 23) sts. When same length as back, shape shoulder as for back.

LEFT FRONT

Work to correspond to right front, reversing rib pat at center front, pocket placement and all shaping, with k2tog instead of ssk on neck shaping.

SLEEVES

With 2 strands A and 1 strand B, cast on 22 (22, 26, 26, 26) sts. Work in k2, p2 rib for 3"/7.5cm. Work in St st inc 1 st each side every other row 2 (4, 1, 2, 2) times, every 4th row 11 (10, 11, 11, 11) times—48 (50, 50, 52, 52) sts. Work even until piece measures 19"/48cm from beg. Bind off.

FINISHING

Block pieces to measurements. Sew shoulder seams.

Neckband

With 2 strands A and 1 strand B and circular needle, pick up and k 134 (138, 142, 146, 150) sts evenly around front and neck edges. Place

THE NEW ENGLANDERS

(Continued from page 141)

markers for 4 evenly spaced buttonholes on left front. **Row 1 (WS)** P2, *k2, p2; rep from * to end. Cont in rib as established for 1 row. **Next row** Work in rib forming 4 buttonholes opposite markers by k2tog, yo for each buttonhole. Cont in rib until band measures 1½"/4cm. Bind off in rib. Sew pocket linings to inside. Place markers at 10¾ (11, 11, 11½, 11½)"/27.5 (28, 28, 29, 29)cm down from shoulders. Sew sleeves to armholes between markers. Sew side and sleeve seams. Sew on buttons.

MEN'S CARDIGAN

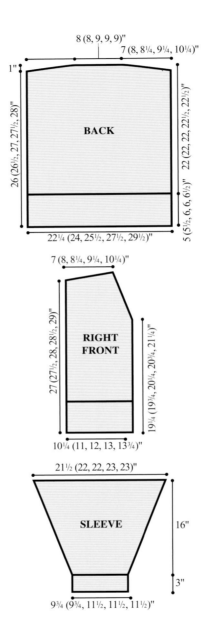

Resources

UNITED STATES RESOURCES

Adrienne Vittadini
distributed by JCA, Inc.

Anny Blatt
7796 Boardwalk
Brighton, MI 48116

Artful Yarns
distributed by JCA, Inc.

Aurora Yarn
PO Box 3068
Moss Beach, CA 94038

Baabajoes Wool Company
PO Box 26064
Lakewood, CO 80226

Brown Sheep Yarn Co.
100662 County Road 16
Mitchell, NE 69357

Cherry Tree Hills Yarns
PO Box 659
Barton, VT 05822

Classic Elite Yarns
300A Jackson Street
Lowell, MA 01852

Cleckheaton
distributed by Plymouth Yarns

Colinette Yarns
distributed by Unique Kolours

Di Vé
distributed by LBUSA

Filatura di Crosa
distributed byTahki•Stacy Charles, Inc.

GGH
distributed by Muench Yarns, Inc.

Garnstudio
distributed by Aurora Yarns

JCA, Inc.
35 Scales Lane
Townsend, MA 01469

KFI
35 Debevoise Ave.
Roosevelt, NY 11575

Karabella yarns
1201 Broadway
New York, NY 10001

LBUSA
PO Box 217
Colorado Springs, CO 80903

Lion Brand Yarn Co.
34 West 15th Street
New York, NY 10011

Mission Falls
distributed by Unique Kolours

Muench Yarns
285 Bel Marin Keys Blvd.
Unit J
Novato, CA 94949-5724

Naturally
distributed by S. R. Kertzer, Ltd.

Plymouth Yarns
PO Box 28
Bristol, PA 19007

Reynolds
distributed by JCA

Rowan Yarns
4 Townsend West, Unit 8
Nashua, NH 03063

Skacel Collection, Inc.
PO Box 88110
Seattle, WA 98138-2110

S.R. Kertzer, Ltd.
105A Wings Road
Woodbridge, ON L4L 6C2

Tahki Yarns
distributed by Glendale, NY 11385

Tahki•Stacy Charles, Inc.
8000 Cooper Ave.
Brooklyn, NY 11222

Tawny
distributed by LBUSA

Unique Kolours
1428 Oak Lane
Downingtown, PA 19335

Woolpak Yarns NZ
distributed by Baabajoes Wool Company

CANADIAN RESOURCES

Aurora Yarns
PO Box 28553
Aurora, ON L4G 6S6

Berroco, Inc.
distributed by S. R. Kertzer, Ltd.

Classic Elite Yarns
distributed by S. R. Kertzer, Ltd.

Cleckheaton
distributed by Diamond Yarn

Diamond Yarn
9697 St. Laurent
Montreal, PQ H3L 2N1 and
155 Martin Ross, Unit #3
Toronto, ON M3J 2L9

Les Fils Muench, Canada
5640 rue Valcourt
Brossard, PQ J4W 1C5

Muench Yarns, Inc.
distributed by Les Fils Muench, Canada

Naturally
distributed by S. R. Kertzer, Ltd.

Patons®
PO Box 40
Listowel, ON N4W 3H3

Rowan
distributed by Diamond Yarn

S. R. Kertzer, Ltd.
105A Winges Rd.
Woodbridge, ON L4L 6C2

We have made every effort to ensure the accuracy of the contents of this publication.
We are not responsible for any human or typographical errors.